THE CAUSE OF
ACCOMPLISHMENT

HELPING BUSINESSES CLIMB THE ELUSIVE LADDER OF **SEO SUCCESS**

DENNIS LANGLAIS

PRAISE

35 + years of friendship Dennis can be summed up in one word, "now". He's been a guiding light for me with an insistence on realizing your potential and not robbing the world of what you can offer to it. To act now means to take charge and make progress. You can't sit still as a friend of Dennis'. The quick call or text is a light switch for action. He has a toolkit of ways to get you to realize the potential he sees in you and is likely frustrated that you're not truly sharing with the world. Do it now. Dennis is on it for you and I'm grateful for the pushes for so many years.

- Scott Moroney

"Dennis Langlais truly embodies the saying that whatever the mind of man can conceive and believe, can be achieved. His book is a master class blueprint to achieve success in whichever field of life you apply his experience & philosophy"
- Alessandra DeFiori

Steven Covey said "As you climb the ladder of success, be sure it's leaning against the right wall" I consider this book as one of the the right walls that will help you set up the right goals and works toward them with Determination, as Dennis Langlais depicts and portrays throw a thorough narrative of his story and experience as the

RANKINGMASTERY

Champion in Sport and Business. Knowing Dennis Langlais and reading his book is like watching a movie then reading the novel that the movie was based on. True Story, Genuine Advice, and Honest Messenger of Success, Personal Growth and Business development...this is a business book, but it talks more about human psychology during the journey...Dennis has been there and done that, in the book he is walking you through the process step by step giving all you the tools you need to get going on your Journey and attain your Personal Goals or Business Goals.

- Najib Chafiq

Figure 1.1:

COPYRIGHT

Copyright © 2023

Book also available at your local bookstore ,or may be ordered by visiting: Dennis Langlais. This material may be protected by copyright. Certainly, here is a recreated sample for your book, "RankingMastery - The Cause Of Accomplishment": Copyright © 2023 by Dennis Langlais Published in the United States by: RankingMastery Press: rankingmastery.com Cover design: Dennis Langlais: illustrations: Dennis Langlais Cover photography: Dennis Langlais All rights reserved. No part of this book may be reproduced in any form or by any electronic or mechanical means including information storage and retrieval systems, without permission in writing from the publisher, except by a reviewer, who may quote brief passages in a review. The content of this book is intended to provide helpful and informative material on the subjects addressed. The author and publisher are not engaged in rendering professional services in the book, and the strategies contained herein may not be suitable for every individual or situation. This book is not intended to be a substitute for professional advice where required. The author and publisher specifically disclaim any liability, loss, or risk, personal or otherwise, which is incurred as a consequence, directly or indirectly, of the use and application of any of the contents of this book.

CONTENTS

THE CAUSE OF	1
ACCOMPLISHMENT	1
HELPING BUSINESSES	1
CLIMB THE ELUSIVE LADDER OF	1
SEO SUCCESS	1
DENNIS LANGLAIS	1
CONTENTS	5
Dedication	9
Foreword	10
Preface	12
Introduction	15
From BMX Stunts to Digital Expertise	18
Family and Friends	20
The Luckiest	23
Pedaling from the Start	28
The Violin	32
See Page Two	35
See Page Two	38
The Evolution of Engagement - Finding Your Page Two	41
Transition and Transformation	44
Failure, Failure, AND Failure...	47
Birth of FIVE Minute Bark	52

Learning the Art of Persistence	55
What's it Matter To You	58
Your Persistent Self	61
Treasure Map Mode	64
Tuning Into Your Journey	67
Treasure Map Mode: Immerse and Embrace	69
Faith and Super-Natural Faith: A Guided Exploration	71
From BMX to Brand Ambassadorship	74
Mastering the Fundamentals of SEO Webpage Structure	77
Mastering the Fundamentals of SEO Webpage Structure	80
Societal Hierarchies and More Hands	84
Win-Win Ranking In Search is Money Today and Tomorrow	87
More Hands in the Room	90
The "Avatar"	92
Traditional Websites, Sales Funnels, SEO Landing Pages	95
The Blend of SEO Key Phrases With Sales	98
The Blend of SEO Key Phrases With Sales	101
Creating Your First Website Landing Pages	103
What Would You Do With An Extra $4600?	106
Embracing A Philosophy	109
From Face-to-Face to Digital Marketing	111
Mining Keywords: Unearth the Phrases Your Customers Are Searching For	114
Beyond the Search Bar: Leveraging Hidden Opportunities in Your Keyword Treasure Trove	116
Samples Of Creating SEO Sales Content For Your Webpage	119
The Cause of Accomplishment	122

The Dirt is in the Details	125
The 15%...	128
AI: Un real, Remarkable, Beyond Belief	131
Business Profiler	134
Are you an Expert or Side Gig	137
Weaving Expertise into Your Marketing - The Real-World Rank	140
The Expert's Playbook: Actions that Solidify Authority	143
Taking the Leap: Embracing the Expert Within You	146
Colors and Branding and More	149
The 'Three Second Rule' - Mastering Visual Impact	152
Margin And Padding	155
The Right Images are Assets	158
Harnessing the Photographic Might of Modern Cell Phones	161
Making Connections	164
My Life Translated Into Links	167
Translate Your Life Into Links	170
Phone Contacts	173
Align Yourself With The Right People	175
The Domino Effect of Strategic Connections	179
Why You Should Understand Podcasting	182
The Gift of Being a Podcast Guest	185
Embarking on the Journey of Hosting	186
Stepping Into the Spotlight – My Podcasting Adventure	188
Quality Sound Matters	191
Kickstarting Your Podcast: A Simple Roadmap to the Airwaves	194

Public Speaking And Guest Speaking	197
The stage calls to me	200
Be Playful	203
I Know Practice Makes Perfect	205
Creating Youtube Videos To Support Your Webpages	208
Creating Webinars	211
Finding Your Way	214
Inception of RankingMastery	217
The Online Directory Strategy	218
The Unexpected Turn	221
The Miracle Shower Revelation	223
The Expansion of Possibilities	225
Vision Becomes Reality	229
Expanding Horizons	231
Utilizing New Platforms for Growth	234
Addressing Client Needs and Software Limitations	237
Introduction To RankingMastery Software Platform	240
Conclusion	246
Our Journey Together	249
The Final Chapter of this Book	251
Acknowledgments	253
About The Author	255

DEDICATION

To my family and friends, thank you for always being there for me, no matter how wild or crazy my ideas got. Each of you has been a huge part of my journey. Being an entrepreneur isn't easy, and you've all seen that up close.

A special shoutout to my mom, who always believed in me and knew I could do great things.

And to my dad, Nooney, for always to remember "what is" and stay focused on the end goals in life. And to all my close friends who called daily to share each day of our lives together. These small things all matter to me.

FOREWORD

When I first met Dennis Langlais back in 2005, I quickly realized he had a special talent in the world of digital marketing, particularly in getting websites to rank high. Over the years, our friendship has grown, and we've worked together on many projects. Among them, RankingMastery really stands out.

RankingMastery isn't just another online tool. It's the result of Dennis's years of hard work and smart thinking about how to do well in the tough world of online business. This book is an extension of that work, and it's here to teach you how to get your website noticed.

I've seen RankingMastery develop from the start. Dennis's way of doing things is both careful and creative. He takes what we know works and mixes it with new, bold ideas. This approach makes RankingMastery different in an industry where new fads come and go quickly.

What's great about this book is how Dennis makes complicated things easy to understand. Whether you're new to online marketing or have been in it for a while, the advice in this book is straightforward and ready to use. These aren't just theories; these are proven ways to do better online.

More than anything, Dennis wants to help people succeed. That's clear in how this book is written. It's like a step-by-step guide, each part building on the last, helping you to really get good at marketing your business or yourself online.

In a world where being online is key to success, the advice Dennis offers is really important. This book is a mix of all his experience, giving you practical tips and a clear plan for how to do well in digital marketing.

I invite you to jump into the world of RankingMastery with this book. It's a chance to learn about improving your online presence, whether it's your website's ranking, your marketing skills, or just understanding how online search works. This book has got you covered.

To wrap up, I want to say a big thanks to Dennis for not only making RankingMastery but also for sharing all his knowledge in this book. It's a real help for anyone looking to make it in the online world.

Blair Williams, Managing Partner, Chugger Software Labs, LLC

PREFACE

In the journey of life and learning, I've come to realize that true disasters often stem not from the moment of catastrophe, but from the unseen events that quietly unfold upstream. This realization mirrors the idea in 'The Butterfly Effect,' where a simple flutter can escalate into a powerful storm. It's a metaphor that beautifully illustrates how small beginnings can lead to monumental outcomes. This understanding led me to contemplate the 'Cause of Accomplishment' – the small yet significant actions that lead to great successes.

My path to accomplishment began with modest yet pivotal moments: the flicker of a TV screen, a tennis ball rebounding against concrete, a balance on a bike, and the thrill of air rushing past as I soared high above a ramp. These instances, seemingly minor, were the first flutters of the butterfly's wings in my life's journey.

Writing "RankingMastery: The Cause of Accomplishment" has been a continuation of this butterfly effect, setting in motion a cascade of events and insights that have further defined my path. This book is not just a recounting of past experiences; it's an active part of my journey, shaping my present and future. Herein, I share not just stories but catalysts for change and understanding, hoping to inspire you with the belief that every action, no matter its size, can create something extraordinary.

This book goes beyond being a mere guide; it's a narrative woven from persistence, insights, and a testament to the human spirit's capacity for accomplishment. As its architect, I offer not only the fruits of my experiences but also the roots – the trials, errors, and revelations that have shaped my understanding of success in both life and the digital realm. The lessons drawn here are from real, hands-on struggles and triumphs that define true mastery.

Within these pages, you will find a duality of purpose. On one hand, it serves as a comprehensive guide for navigating the competitive landscape of online ranking, reflecting my life's work in developing software that aids businesses in achieving SEO success. On the other hand, it is a tapestry of personal narratives, each illustrating broader success principles applicable to personal growth and beyond.

The stories I share are reflections of the universal human experience, tales of those who dared to want more from life, who discovered within themselves a relentless drive to excel. From the rhythmic echo of a tennis ball in a childhood basement to the adrenaline-fueled highs above a BMX ramp, these experiences have marked my journey to understanding accomplishment.

"RankingMastery" is about mastering the art of ranking, not just in the realms of search engines but also in life's many endeavors. This book reveals how the principles that propel websites to the top are similar to those that can elevate our lives: focus, attention to detail, discipline, and the courage to keep pushing forward.

As you delve into this book, I invite you to engage with the material actively. Reflect on your own experiences, draw parallels to your ambitions, and consider the questions it poses. Will you choose to be a mere participant, or will you strive to rank among the accomplished?

Welcome to "RankingMastery: The Cause of Accomplishment." Let's embark on this journey together.

INTRODUCTION

THE AUTHOR'S JOURNEY

From the relentless, freezing practices on ramps and pavement in the streets of Northbridge, Massachusetts, to the global stage, Dennis Langlais' BMX journey embodies passion, innovation, and resilience. In the 1980s, while BMX Racing captivated many, it was the allure of BMX Freestyle that seized Dennis's heart. His unwavering dedication, even through the harshest Northeastern winters, signaled a passion that went far beyond a fleeting hobby.

Dennis's journey was never solely about mastering tricks on pedals. It encompassed winning, influenced by his mother, and innovation, inspired by his father. This was blended with leadership skills and an understanding of the significance of influence and positioning. As Dennis transitioned from a young enthusiast to a prominent force in the BMX world, he realized the power of ranking and influence. His collaborations with major brands and his ability to attract them towards BMX freestyle were not mere chances but a testament to his understanding of positioning and influence.

His early efforts, including being a rider on the 'East Coast Wheels Team' and competing at a high level in the AFA

Freestyle competition series, showcased his innate ability to recognize and seize opportunities. These ventures were precursors to larger collaborations, such as being a part of Ron Stebenne's masterful creation of the iconic Mountain Dew/GT Team, a significant stepping stone that elevated him to new levels of branding and recognition.

Reflecting on Dennis's career trajectory in Freestyle BMX, one might ponder the direction it might have taken without Ron Stebenne, the architect of the infamous 'Mountain Dew GT Trick Team'. Stebenne's contributions to the riders went far beyond mere dedication. He made a significant leap, leaving his secure job as an influential 6th-grade teacher, to guide them into becoming the world-renowned 'Mountain Dew GT Trick Team'. To this day, few organizations have been seen to run with such precision, niche focus, and professionalism. Stebenne's leadership and vision have undoubtedly shaped the lives of many riders, imparting lessons and values that extend well beyond the ramps and BMX tracks.

Yet, the BMX Freestyle circuits were just the beginning for Dennis. After moving to San Diego, he showcased another facet of his genius: his tech-savviness. The inception of a multifunctional website that automated the operations of his school assembly enterprise signified his grasp of the digital age's potentials. This venture was more than just a business—it was a testament to Dennis's understanding of influence and rank in the digital realm.

Today, Dennis Langlais stands not just as a BMX legend but as a visionary who understands the essence of positioning oneself, whether on the BMX Extreme Sports stage or the vast expanse of the internet. His journey, from pedals to pixels, provides invaluable lessons on the importance of influence, ranking, and leveraging one's unique experiences to carve a niche in any arena.

Figure 1.2:

FROM BMX STUNTS TO DIGITAL EXPERTISE

As I leaf through the mental scrapbook of my past, the transition from the innocent zeal of stickball games to the gritty BMX tracks seems almost predestined. Back then, as a kid growing up, I was consumed by one thing: my BMX bike. It wasn't the applause or the adulation that drove me—it was the wind against my face, the freedom, the pure joy of riding. From the somewhat obscure BMX scene of my corner in the U.S., I didn't just participate; I pioneered, elevating our local passion to a global phenomenon.

Years later, the world would start to buzz with the term "influencer," a notion that had no name during my formative BMX Freestyle days. As I ventured into the world of business, I began to realize something striking. Those days of hitting to ramp hard, the teams I built, the community we fostered—these weren't just relics of my youth. They were a treasure trove of experience and authenticity in a world craving real stories and genuine heroes. And I was sitting on a goldmine of experiences without even realizing it.

You might think reflecting on all the opportunities that slipped by could have left me with regrets, pondering the millions that might have been. But that's not how I saw it. To me, it was a clear signal of a new opportunity, a second act. The young guy who once lived for the thrill of BMX was now making his mark in the world of business. My narrative expanded beyond BMX freestyle; it now included insights and inspirations for anyone starting their journey, for anyone who's ever dared to dream.

FAMILY AND FRIENDS

WHEN WE WERE KIDS

Childhood, that magical time when imagination knows no bounds and every day holds the promise of a new adventure, was especially memorable for us. Our days were chapters of an unwritten book, each activity a story in itself, enough to fill volumes with the exploits and escapades of youth. We had an annual cycle, a rhythm to our madness, dictated by the seasons and our boundless energy.

Summer was the domain of stickball, a game chosen as much for the thrill of the sport as for the safety of our neighbors' windows. The Salmon family's yard became our stadium, their lawn the field where legends were born and rivalries were settled. We swapped the traditional baseball for a small rubber ball and a slender bat, a perfect adaptation to our suburban landscape. The game was simple, but it was ours, a testament to our ingenuity and resourcefulness.

As the leaves began to change, so did our sports. Football and basketball dominated, with the creation of a neighborhood league that had us competing against other parts of town, other boroughs. We weren't just kids; we were athletes in the making, each game a step towards something greater.

But it was BMX Racing and Freestyle that truly captured our hearts. With fervor and seriousness, we carved a track into the earth itself, right next to my home, where an old, abandoned house once stood. We crafted jumps and berms with our own hands, our shovels carving out a place for our passion. This track, complete with its own drainage system, was a marvel of childhood engineering, a testament to what kids can do when driven by passion and a touch of youthful audacity.

However, it wasn't all sport and games. With the arrival of autumn came the season of acorn wars, a time when things turned a tad more anarchic. We would gather acorns by the bagful, hoarding them like precious ammunition, preparing for the neighborhood skirmish that had become an annual tradition. Our battlegrounds were the same streets where we raced our bikes and played our games, now transformed into arenas of friendly but fierce competition.

Looking back, it's astounding to think of the freedom and creativity we wielded as children. To imagine a group of young teens today undertaking such projects might seem far-fetched, yet we did it. We were architects of our own entertainment, constructors of our own childhood lore. We didn't just live in our neighborhood; we shaped it with our games, our races, and our laughter.

These memories are more than just nostalgia; they are a reminder of a time when life was simpler, yet somehow richer. We were indeed the luckiest, for in our youthful endeavors, we found joy, camaraderie, and the pure, unabated thrill of being alive.

Figure 1.4:

Family and Friends

THE LUCKIEST

Every journey has its genesis, often nestled in the comfort of a place we call home. Mine took root in my grandmother's house in Rockdale, Massachusetts. It was there, in that humble abode where Sunday mornings were sacred and the pre-church hours were woven with familiar love, that my story began. My grandmother's home was a sanctuary of warmth, where the simplest pleasures—like the unrivaled taste of her homemade bread and the comfort of her welcoming arms—made me feel cherished, like the most significant person in her world.

My grandmother was more than a relative; she was a mentor in the games of checkers and chess, a co-conspirator in bouts of Connect Four, and a generous soul who never hesitated to spoil me. Our connection was as strong as the strategy games we played for hours, a bond forged through indulgence and shared joy. Yet, amidst the spoiling, it was in the simplicity of her living room, with the soundtrack of a baseball game filling the air, that a defining moment took shape—a moment that's as vivid today as it was back then.

I was but four years old, and the world seemed as vast as the expanse of my grandmother's couch. The Red Sox game flickering on the TV presented a tableau of vibrant greens and stark whites and reds, a captivating contrast that drew me in. The athletes, clad in their uniforms, were like gallant figures in a child's imaginative play, and the electrifying energy of the crowd reached out from the screen, stirring a deep sense of awe within me. That day, a dream was born: to be a baseball player. This wasn't a fleeting wish of a young boy but the seed of an aspiration that would grow to inform my future endeavors.

Those Sunday mornings with my grandmother laid the foundation for my pursuits in athletics and entrepreneurship. She taught me more than just games; she instilled in me the value of chasing one's dreams, a lesson that I would carry with me throughout life. Her faith in me was unwavering, even in tasks as mundane as fetching milk from Cumberland Farms or cigarettes from the local mom-and-pop shop for a mere quarter.

Looking back, I see how fortunate I was. Not just for a grandmother's indulgence, but for a family that nurtured my aspirations from their inception. The Langlais way was not one of grand gestures or overt expressions of affection—we were not a family of bear hugs or tearful goodbyes. Yet, the love was there, implicit in every action, every shared silence. We were taught the value of loyalty and service, the sort that meant picking up a friend from the airport at 4 AM without a second thought. We were raised with big hearts and few words.

Each family member's life was a chapter in my education, a series of living lessons on what to embrace and what to avoid. My father's weekly hikes, the neighborhood excursions to Ted's for penny candy—these were the threads in the fabric of my childhood. Bazooka gum, Tootsie Rolls, jellyfish candies—they weren't just treats; they were the currency of carefree days and the sweetness of life's simple joys.

My mother, the matriarch of creativity in our family, is a woman whose life's work could easily fill the pages of a book—a vibrant collage titled "Arts and Crafts For Life." Her ingenuity and artistic flair infused our home with a spirit of creation, and it's from her that I inherited the imaginative essence that breathes life into my software designs. Where my father provided the structured engineering mindset, my mother brought color, form, and boundless possibility.

Her world was one of ceaseless creation, where the ordinary transformed into the extraordinary under her touch. She taught me to see the hidden potential in everything, from the wild vines heavy with grapes in the untamed corners of Northbridge, destined to become jars of sweet jelly, to the ripe apples that would be the soul of her homemade pies. Tomatoes plucked fresh from the vine were not just fruit; they were the beginning of a sauce that spoke of home.

To this day, she's a whirlwind of activity, her second-floor sanctuary a treasure trove of ongoing projects. There, amidst the kaleidoscope of stained glass waiting to catch the light, diamond dot portraits that dazzle the eye, and even masks sewn during the pandemic—a testament to her blend of practicality and artistry—she crafts endlessly. Her generosity knows no bounds, creating keepsakes for everyone in her orbit, yet rarely anything solely for herself.

Her culinary prowess was another canvas for her creativity. Dishes like American chop suey and shepherd's pie were not mere meals; they were experiences, each bite a flavor of comfort, a memory of home. A dash of salt, a hint of pepper, and it was 'go time'—a call to the table that always meant more than just food; it meant family, it meant love, it meant home.

In her, I saw the joy of making, the happiness that comes not from material wealth but from the act of creation and sharing. My mother's zest for crafting and cooking, her instinct for turning the raw into the refined, subtly sculpted my approach to software—not just as a tool but as a tapestry of code and design, waiting to bring joy and utility to those who would use it.

Her influence is a thread that runs through the fabric of my professional life, a reminder that at the heart of innovation lies a love for creation and a desire to bring something new into the world. Her legacy is not just in the stained glass that dances with the daylight or the food that nourishes but in the lessons of creativity, generosity, and passion that continue to inspire my journey.

Figure 1.5:

PEDALING FROM THE START

THE STREETS OF NORTHBRIDGE MASSACHUSETTS

The '80s. Man, what a time. Everything was electric, buzzing with this sort of youthful energy that just beckoned you to be a part of something bigger. In the heart of Massachusetts, that "something" for me was BMX.

I can still feel it - that unmistakable roar of tires gripping onto a well-worn wooden quarter-pipe ramp. Launching myself skyward, reaching nearly 20 feet off the ground, was like defying gravity. For a few heartbeats, the world below just blurred, while the wind roared past, its fierce rush almost outdoing the raw beats of Run DMC from my trusty boombox.

But it wasn't just the adrenaline - although, trust me, that was addictive. BMX was freedom, expression, a statement. While many of my buddies were getting into the regular routines of suburbia, I needed more. I found a tribe in the BMX community; a wild bunch who spoke my language of thrills and spills.

And spills there were - plenty of them. Scraped knees, elbows, a bruised ego or two. But every time I bit the dust, it only amped up my drive. Each tumble wasn't a setback; it was a lesson, pushing me to understand my limits and then dare to cross them.

As the streets of Massachusetts morphed into bigger, more challenging arenas, my love for BMX wasn't just a weekend fling anymore - it was who I was. Before I knew it, I was rubbing shoulders, or rather handlebars, with some of the best out there. From a kid with a dream on that rickety ramp in Massachusetts, with good ol' Run DMC setting the backdrop to my life, I was on the global stage, carving out a path for others to follow.

This journey, with all its highs and lows, wasn't just about BMX; it was about a kid's burning passion, his undying perseverance, and an unyielding chase of dreams. Dreams that started with a jump, a beat, and a will to soar.

From the bustling streets of Massachusetts to the grand arenas of the world, my BMX journey transcended any boundary I had ever envisioned. My roots were anchored with Scott Moroney, Matt Salmon, Tony Peloquin, and the imaginative Jeff Larson. Their influence had given me wings, but the time had come for me to soar even higher. The call from Ron Stebenne with news that GT BMX Team Manager Wanted Me Dennis to go on World Tour with Martin Aparijo.

It wasn't easy parting ways with my friends, with those familiar alleyways and ramps that witnessed my growth as a BMX rider. Yet, the allure of an international audience and the promise of new terrains beckoned.

Each country we touched brought its own rhythm, culture, and set of challenges. England and Ireland were a blur of historic streets and verdant landscapes, both equally thrilling backdrops for our BMX escapades. The scents of France will forever be etched in my mind: the combination of fresh croissants and the unique smell of our rubber tires burning against cobblestone streets.

In Paris, Martin and I became urban explorers, dashing through its iconic streets, using every curb and staircase as a launchpad for our stunts. The French Riviera was an experience in itself; hours spent riding the boardwalks, the salty sea breeze challenging our balance, and the azure waters inviting us after a day's hard work. We'd push the boundaries, taking hands or feet off mid-air, introducing spins and twists, always aiming to elevate our performances.

Our scheduled autograph sessions turned into unexpected platforms of connection. It wasn't just about signing posters or merchandise; it was about the intimate conversations that followed. Eager fans and fellow BMX enthusiasts shared their own tales, exchanged notes on the latest tricks, and dreamed aloud about the future of BMX. The shared anticipation of what the sport could evolve into was palpable in every interaction.

Beyond the adrenaline and the performances, the tour was a tapestry of moments: from forging bonds with people from different walks of life to reminiscing about our journey while overlooking a Swiss valley or while relaxing on a Venezuelan beach.

The GT BMX World Tour wasn't just a series of shows. It was a journey of friendships, experiences, lessons, and above all, an affirmation that our shared love for BMX united us, irrespective of language, culture, or borders. Every jump, twist, and turn was a testament to our shared passion and a promise of greater adventures ahead.

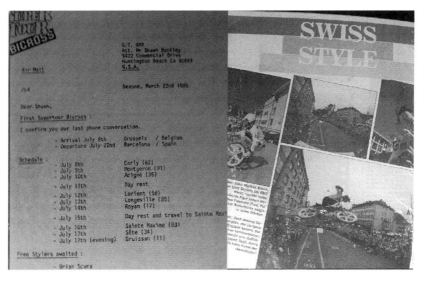

Figure 1.6:

Pedaling from the Start

THE VIOLIN

As life unfolds, we often find moments to reflect with those who have been part of our journey. These moments, a blend of past experiences and present insights, are both invaluable and enlightening. It's November 3rd, 2023. A crisp chill in the air accompanies my drive towards downtown San Diego. Behind the wheel of my new Mercedes GLC AMG 63 – a symbol of my resilience through tough times – I relish brief bursts of acceleration. This 470 horsepower marvel roars with a symphony of raw power and sheer exhilaration, a sound so addictive it encapsulates the thrill of each drive. Here, amidst the vibrant pulse of the city, the past and future are set to converge. Matt, better known as 'M Craze' from the days when BMX bikes were our chariots and asphalt our arena, is arriving for a conference. However, this meeting isn't just any ordinary catch-up; it represents the rekindling of a shared spark, a mentality forged on the sun-baked streets of Northbridge, Massachusetts..

Matt now helms the family business, but the title of CEO doesn't eclipse the streak of that thrill-seeking kid I knew. He's in town for a 'family business conference,' yet the familial ties under discussion extend beyond bloodlines—it's about the family of life, those you pick up along the way who stick because you vibrate on the same frequency.

As we drive towards Del Mar to find 'The Brig,' a local coastal restaurant, we find ourselves at a table overlooking the horse race track, away from the conference's bustle. The conversation naturally deepens. The din of networking fades to a murmur behind us as we lean into familiar territory: the insatiable drive to be more, to do more.

'You know,' Matt muses, swirling a draft beer that catches the dim light like liquid gold after a long day, 'when people want to play the violin, they don't just scratch away and hope for music. They take lessons; they learn from the masters.'

I nod, memories flashing of our younger selves: gritty hands, scabbed knees, and the relentless pursuit of the next big stunt.

'It's the same in business,' he continues. 'Some folks act like they've got it all figured out from the get-go. But it's those who seek out lessons, who aren't afraid to ask for help to hone their craft; they're the ones who really go places.'

I raise my glass, the clink echoing a truth we both know. This is the essence of our bond, a relentless curiosity and the recognition that mastery, in any domain, is a journey of perpetual learning. We'd learned it on the streets, where every skinned knee was a lesson, every landed trick a triumphant chapter in our ongoing story of growth.

As we part that night, a crisp San Diego breeze mingles with the warmth of reconnection. I realize that the streets of Northbridge hadn't just given us a playground. They'd given us a mindset—the 'M Craze' mentality—that unquenchable desire to push boundaries and the wisdom to seek out the maestros of our ambitions.

Whether in the echo of a violin hall or the cutthroat silence of the boardroom, it's this symphony of lessons learned and shared that composes the overture to success.

SEE PAGE TWO

THE DAWN OF DIGITAL MARKETING FOR MY BMX SCHOOL ASSEMBLIES COMPANY

In the nascent days of my BMX School Assemblies Company, long before the digital sunrise had illuminated the landscape of marketing, our strategies were confined to the tangible and the immediate. Our outreach efforts were grounded in the physical—mass mailings that we hoped would land in welcoming hands, cold calls that would break through the ice of reception, and in-person visits where our enthusiasm and presence would fill the room just as much as our promotional materials did.

Among these traditional tactics, fax broadcasting emerged as a novel and somewhat controversial technique. At the time, it was our version of email marketing—a direct line to our potential customers, the schools. But, as with any form of disruptive technology, it was met with mixed reactions. "You're wasting our paper," some would say, voicing the early echoes of today's concerns over digital spam. Yet, despite its detractors, the effectiveness of fax broadcasting was undeniable. For every complaint about wasted paper, there were calls of interest, schools intrigued by the prospect of hosting our BMX spectacle.

The setup for our fax broadcasting operation was something of a technological ballet. I managed to acquire several Macintosh computers, each equipped with a built-in fax card—a rarity at the time. These machines became our tireless night-shift workers. We would line up seven phone lines, orchestrating them to dispatch our faxes in the quiet hours of the night. As we slept, our messages were whisked away through the phone lines, casting our net far and wide.

The next morning, we'd be greeted by the hum of anticipation, the office abuzz with the possibility of returned interest. And sure enough, the calls would come in—schools on the other end of the line, wanting to bring the thrill of BMX stunts to their students.

Each affirmative response was a nugget of gold, a validation of our efforts and a promise of an engaged audience for our riders.

This was a time when technology began to redefine what was possible in marketing. It was a glimpse into a future where our reach could extend far beyond what our physical presence could manage—a future where marketing could happen as we slept, where our messages could find their way without us having to guide them every step of the journey. It was, in every sense, the precursor to the digital marketing revolution that would soon take hold, forever changing the way we connected with our audiences.

SEE PAGE TWO

Sometimes, the most valuable treasures are unearthed entirely by chance, a serendipitous find that only in hindsight seems like it was marked on a map. It was on one such occasion that 'Treasure Map Mode' came into play before I had even named the concept. We were constantly fine-tuning our sales copy, always looking for that alchemy of words that would turn interest into bookings.

Then came the day that would change our strategy altogether. In a flurry of activity and a rush against time, I set the faxes to send. It was a routine I had performed countless times, but in my haste, I made a blunder. The second page, the one with all the critical details and the call to action, was left behind. As the machines hummed through the night, dispatching page one of our promotional material to 15,000 faxes, the second page lay forgotten.

The next morning, I braced myself for the fallout of this costly mistake, expecting silence or at best, confusion. But the reality was far from it. The calls began to trickle in, then pour—a deluge of inquiries and requests for the elusive 'page two.' The secretaries from schools were on the line, their curiosity piqued by the absence of information. What we anticipated to be a disaster turned into an unprecedented engagement.

This unexpected twist led to an epiphany. What if the call to action wasn't just about providing information but about creating an intrigue? What if we intentionally invited our audience to seek out 'page two'? We decided to test this hypothesis, intentionally printing "See Page Two" in bold at the bottom of the first page, fully knowing there was no second page to be found.

The result? The mystery of the missing page worked like a charm, drawing more calls and interest than any of our previous, meticulously detailed faxes. It was a moment of clarity, a realization that sometimes the map you're following has invisible contours that can only be revealed through unexpected turns.

This was 'Treasure Map Mode' in action—navigating not with a clear X marking the spot, but with the intuition that something valuable lay just beyond the visible path. It was a lesson in marketing, in human psychology, and in the power of curiosity. From that day forward, we embraced the allure of the unknown, the potential of a story half-told, the power of a journey not fully charted. And just like that, a mistake was transformed into a masterstroke, guiding us to a treasure trove of engagement and success.

Figure 1.7:

See Page Two

THE EVOLUTION OF ENGAGEMENT - FINDING YOUR PAGE TWO

As the marketing landscape evolved, so too did the tactics we employed to reach our audience. The era of fax broadcasting began to wane, not just because technology advanced, but also because opportunists found a way to exploit the system, turning unsolicited faxes into lawsuits. It was a signal for change, a nudge to pivot and innovate once again. The 'See Page Two' strategy had served its purpose, but it was time to translate that lesson into the new age of digital marketing.

The question then became, "What's your Page Two?" In a world brimming with content, where every click brings a barrage of information, how do you create that intrigue, that compelling cliffhanger that makes your audience seek more? In this digital era, your Page Two is the element that captivates, that holds a promise of more—more information, more value, more engagement.

The concept of hitting your client over the head with a bat to get their attention may sound extreme, but it's a metaphor for the impact you need to make in a sea of distractions. Your Page Two doesn't need to be a physical page; it could be the teaser video that leaves viewers wanting more, the blog post that ends with a provocative question, or the social media post that hints at a compelling story, driving traffic to your website for the full reveal.

In 'Treasure Map Mode', you're always on the lookout for that Page Two—the hook that keeps your audience engaged. It's about understanding the journey you want your audience to take and creating a trail of digital breadcrumbs that leads them to the next step. Whether that's a sign-up form, a download button for a white paper, or a teaser for an upcoming webinar, it should be something that entices a click, a read, a listen, a watch.

Today, your Page Two might take many forms. It could be an exclusive offer that's unlocked with a subscription, a webinar that promises to reveal industry secrets, or an interactive tool that adds value to your users' experience. The essence of Page Two is the art of keeping your audience's journey alive, providing them with a clear and enticing path forward.

In your 'Treasure Map Mode', consider your current strategies. Are you giving your audience enough to get them interested but not everything up front? Are you creating opportunities for engagement that lead them on a journey deeper into your brand's narrative? What's the bat that will get their attention, and what's the Page Two that will keep it?

As you adapt to the new marketing schemes that the digital era demands, remember the success of your fax broadcasts. The core principle remains the same: capture attention and maintain engagement. Your challenge is to find your modern Page Two, to innovate within the digital space, and to create a treasure hunt that your audience is eager to embark upon.

TRANSITION AND TRANSFORMATION

NON-COMPETE AGREEMENTS

Following the sale of my company, I found myself bound by a three-year non-compete agreement, which meant I had to start from scratch, learning a new trade and finding a different source of income. I explored numerous avenues, trying various approaches, but my efforts often led to dead ends. Faced with financial uncertainty, I eventually circled back to what I knew best—an endeavor that was as familiar as the back of my hand—the BMX school assembly business.

I was well-versed in the mechanics of running that business; it was almost second nature to me, a guaranteed source of income. However, the challenge lay in starting anew. How could I rebuild from the ground up? How could I quickly generate leads to get back on my feet? The answer hit me like a bolt of lightning: I had always believed that creating a directory could open doors not only for selling bike shows but also for other assemblies that schools cherished.

With a wild idea in my head, I set out to craft this directory. Having honed my programming skills, I was now equipped to handle most of the technical aspects myself. For the heavy lifting, I turned to my invaluable friend, Blair Williams, who had weathered life's ups and downs alongside me. Thankfully, we found ourselves on opposite sides, ready to support each other in times of need. I reached out to him in a panic, explaining my need for a specific algorithm to make this venture work. "Can you do it?" I asked. "Let's give it a try," he replied.

Together, we tinkered with code for hours on end, and suddenly, there it was—the secret sauce! I quickly hired anyone I could afford and gathered competitors in the school assembly business, adding them to the directory. It was an exhilarating accomplishment, but now it was time to attract leads. Little did I know that an unexpected twist awaited me.

My plan was to gather leads and sell them to acts for a mere $10, knowing their true worth was much higher. However, an unforeseen challenge emerged. One cold January morning in 2018, I woke up in San Diego to find cease and desist letters from not just one, but several acts. They were furious that I had included them in my directory, and what was worse, the pages I had created were ranking higher on Google than their own websites. They didn't take kindly to that.

Emotionally and financially, I was at my breaking point. It felt like the final nail in the coffin. But then, as I stood in the shower, a thought crossed my mind: "If these pages are ranking higher than their own websites, why not modify this for someone who could see the value in this apparent disaster?" I incorporated the technology into my own websites, and suddenly, leads began pouring in at an astonishing rate. My financial situation was transforming rapidly, and I had stumbled upon an unexpected opportunity in the midst of adversity.

The life lesson I gleaned from this tumultuous period was clear: adversity can be a catalyst for growth and innovation. It taught me the importance of resilience, adaptability, and the unwavering belief that even in the face of seemingly insurmountable challenges, opportunities abound. In the end, it was this very adversity that propelled me forward, leading to the birth of RankingMastery and a newfound purpose—to empower others to find their rightful place in the digital realm.

This chapter serves as a testament to the idea that life's greatest lessons often emerge from its most formidable trials, and that with determination, creativity, and a willingness to embrace change, we can transform adversity into unparalleled opportunity.

Transition and Transformation

FAILURE, FAILURE, AND FAILURE...

Reflecting on my journey, I've navigated through a myriad of challenges and embarked on ambitious endeavors to create software platforms. My initial inspiration was drawn from the success of the software that streamlined my BMX School Shows, a tool that revolutionized efficiency and versatility in my business operations. This experience ignited a desire within me to extend these benefits to others, to craft solutions that would ease the burdens of their professional pursuits.

The Beginning – Inside HOA and Forging Partnerships

Embarking on the development of Inside HOA, I found not just an opportunity to innovate but also a partnership that would shape my future endeavors. It was in this initial venture that I crossed paths with Blair Williams, a web developer whose expertise and dedication were matched only by his patience and resilience. Our collaboration was set against a backdrop of ambition and the shared goal of creating a platform that would serve Homeowners Associations with unprecedented efficiency and transparency.

As is often the case with first ventures, Inside HOA was a learning ground, a project that brought to light the complexities and challenges inherent in bringing a software idea to life. Blair and I grappled with aligning our visions for the platform, and the developmental process was a storm of brainstorming sessions, coding marathons, and the inevitable revisiting of features we thought we had already finalized.

The journey was anything but smooth. My drive to perfect the platform led to a cascade of change requests—each one with the potential to improve the end product but also adding layers of complexity and time to our workload. It tested our limits, pushing Blair's capacity to deliver and my own understanding of the delicate balance between innovation and feasibility.

Despite the hurdles, what stood out was the foundation of mutual respect and open communication that Blair and I had established. Even as Inside HOA faced its share of trials, culminating in a pause that neither of us had anticipated, our professional rapport remained untarnished. The project's hiatus became a silent promise of potential—a belief that our collaboration was not to end here but to be renewed under better circumstances.

Our paths diverged temporarily, yet the respect and the acknowledgment of each other's integrity and skill bound us for future ventures. We both moved forward, gathering further experience, honing our skills, and building our individual portfolios, all the while knowing that the partnership forged during the Inside HOA days was one worth revisiting.

And revisit we did. When the time was right, Blair and I reconnected with a wealth of new insights and a refined approach to collaboration. The misalignments that had once seemed insurmountable now became the stepping stones to a stronger working relationship, one that continues to thrive. Our partnership, tested by the fires of development challenges, emerged stronger, ready to tackle new projects with a deeper understanding and a shared history that enriched our collaborative efforts.

Inside HOA, with all its aspirations and setbacks, was not just a software project. It was the beginning of a professional journey with Blair Williams—a journey marked by discovery, adaptation, and the kind of partnership that becomes all too rare in the fast-paced world of technology. It stands as a testament to the fact that sometimes, the most enduring successes are born from the trials that test us the most.

The inception of Approcessor.com was not just a product of necessity during the housing crisis, but also the result of collaborative inspiration. The idea was sparked by a conversation with a good friend and industry colleague, Jason Stroder. His insights played a pivotal role in shaping the architecture of the platform, ensuring it would directly address the needs of his team and others in the field navigating the complexities of loan modifications.

Our collaboration aimed to create a system that could bring a sense of clarity and control to a process that had left many homeowners in the dark. As the software began to take form, the initial response was overwhelmingly positive. Industry professionals, including Jason and his team, found immense value in Approcessor.com, recognizing its potential to streamline their workflow and provide a transparent service to their clients.

The sight of offices humming with the activity generated by our software was a powerful motivator. To see a concept that originated from a desire to help, now actively being used as an essential business tool, was incredibly affirming. The revenue from brokers and legal professionals who saw the worth in Approcessor.com was a testament to the platform's functionality and relevance.

Yet, the journey of Approcessor.com was met with formidable challenges. The financial investment required to maintain and advance the platform was significant. As the tides of the industry changed and banks began to adapt and simplify their loan modification procedures, the once-clear gap in the market that Approcessor.com filled started to close. The urgency for such a tool diminished, and with it, the sustainability of the business model we had built.

Despite the closeness to completion and the robustness of its design, the shifting market conditions led to a downturn in the viability of Approcessor.com. The financial strain became pronounced, and the project that had begun with high hopes and a strong partnership faced an uncertain future.

But the fire within me wasn't easily extinguished. I ventured next into the real estate domain with a marketing platform designed to enhance the dynamics between agents and homeowners. Though it didn't take off as I had hoped, each interaction, each build, was a lesson learned—a deposit into my bank of experience.

Undeterred, I pivoted again, this time towards a self-help platform that integrated goal-setting tools, leveraging my growing podcast as a complementary medium. Still, success remained elusive, a whisper in the wind that I couldn't quite grasp.

After that endeavor, I vowed to step away from the software world—a vow made in a moment of fatigue, yet not a reflection of my enduring passion for creation and innovation.

In the wake of these experiences, I've come to understand that the path of innovation is rarely linear. It's a journey marked by resilience, a testament to the enduring human spirit that looks adversity in the eye and sees not an end, but an invitation to begin anew. This part of my story is an honest account, a narrative that speaks to the tenacity required to pursue one's vision amidst the unpredictable tides of the tech industry. It's a chronicle of the trials that shape us, the determination that defines us, and the relentless pursuit of the innovation that drives us.

Transition and Transformation

BIRTH OF FIVE MINUTE BARK

Translating raw passion from BMX ramps into the entrepreneurial world wasn't a direct jump—it was a carefully orchestrated sequence of movements, just like my BMX routines. The momentum from my BMX days carried me into the realm of podcasts, leading me to create the "FIVE Minute Bark." Just like how I used to dazzle the audience with my BMX stunts, I now had the platform to captivate listeners with intriguing conversations, and not just with anyone, but with some of the brightest minds in entrepreneurship.

One of the standout conversations was with Russell Brunson, the genius co-owner of ClickFunnels. We delved deep into the world of digital marketing, funnel strategy, and how businesses can exponentially grow online. I had the privilege of hosting Alex Charfen, a prodigious figure who has a penchant for coaching billionaires, making them even more successful. Then there was Steven Weatherford, the NFL's star kicker. His overwhelming passion for fitness was palpable, and our conversation resonated with many, from fitness enthusiasts to those seeking motivation in their lives.

But amidst these podcasts, a realization dawned upon me. Entrepreneurs, especially those just starting out, struggled to navigate the digital landscape. With my history of branding and influence, I recognized a gap—a need for a platform that could simplify online presence and help businesses get discovered in searches.

That led to the inception of RankingMastery, my latest venture and, I daresay, my most ambitious project yet. Drawing from my rich tapestry of experiences—from BMX tracks, world tours, brand endorsements to intimate podcast conversations—I crafted a software platform tailored for entrepreneurs. The essence? To help them build effective websites that not only showcase their business but also ensure they rank high in online searches.

In many ways, RankingMastery is the culmination of all the lessons I've learned over the years. It embodies the passion of my BMX days, the insights from my podcast guests, and the business acumen developed over the years. Now, I'm on a new kind of tour—not on a bike, but with a mission to empower businesses to find their rightful place in the digital realm.

Figure 1.8:

LEARNING THE ART OF PERSISTENCE

THE PRISONER

They say that to truly excel, one must be willing to risk it all. But what separates the reckless gambler from the shrewd strategist is not the willingness to take a leap, but the ability to persist through the inevitable stumbles and falls. In life's high stakes game, prisoners of circumstance are often those who dared greatly, yet found themselves on the wrong side of risk. Within their stories, however, lies a powerful lesson in resilience.

Meet an individual who has hit rock bottom, and you'll find a raw model for persistence. These are the ones who have lost everything—family, friends, money, homes—and yet, there's an undeniable spark within them. Their talents, once unbridled and uncontrolled, could have fueled extraordinary success had they channeled their relentless energy differently.

This chapter asks a pivotal question: How can you harness the kind of relentless pursuit often found in the most unexpected mentors, applying it to the disciplined field of online marketing? How do you uncover the side of yourself that's willing to step out of your comfort zone and execute the strategies shared in this book, to begin mastering SEO and online marketing?

Many fear the fall, the misstep, the possibility of public failure. But without pushing boundaries, without risking those scrapes and tumbles, the successes you dream of remain just that—dreams. In previous chapters, we discussed entering "treasure map mode" and possessing "supernatural faith," both necessary mindsets for taking bold action. But make no mistake, there is no magic wand that transforms your business overnight. What I offer is a map—a collection of tried and tested pathways paved by those who have walked before, stumbled, and risen again.

In your pursuit of online mastery, action is your greatest ally. Yes, you will encounter failure. Each "no," each failed campaign, each SEO strategy that doesn't pan out is similar to a scrape on the knee of your business. But what do we know about scraped knees? They heal. They become tougher. They prepare you for the next play, the next leap.

Do not be dissuaded by the pace of your progress. Whether you move at a tortoise's pace or a hare's sprint, remember: most seminars you attend, books you read, and gurus you follow are offering wisdom distilled from a multitude of failures.

Your path in SEO and online marketing will demand persistence. It will ask you to look at the empty page of your website's analytics and see the potential for a masterpiece. It will call upon you to tweak and refine your keywords, your content, your user experience—not just once, but relentlessly, until the gears of the internet begin to turn in your favor.

And so, this chapter is not just about the how-to of SEO, but about the who-you-must-become to wield these tools effectively. To rank online is to rank within yourself—a hierarchy of traits with persistence sitting firmly at the top. As we move forward, let's explore the practical steps to build this relentless pursuit, one that doesn't end at the first hurdle but sees it as the first of many stepping stones to a success that is both hard-won and deeply satisfying.

Learning the Art of Persistence

WHAT'S IT MATTER TO YOU

Persistence is a canvas painted with the broad strokes of ambition and the fine lines of daily efforts. It's personal. It's intimate. It's the fire that warms you during the cold trials of entrepreneurship and online ventures. But to persist with purpose, you must first answer a critical question: What does it all matter to you?

In the echoing chambers of your deepest whys, you'll find persistence waiting. It's not just about learning the tactics of SEO or mastering the art of online marketing. It's about why you wake up every day and why you're willing to face rejection and failure without losing stride. Why do you do it? What's at stake?

For some, it's the dream of financial freedom; for others, it's the legacy they wish to leave. Maybe it's the thrill of the climb or the joy found in the creation process itself. But until you identify your 'why,' your persistence is merely a hollow shell—impressive to look at but easily shattered.

Consider the entrepreneurs who've made history, the ones whose stories we tell in awe. They knew their 'why.' It wasn't just about building a business; it was about changing the world, providing for their families, or simply proving to themselves that they could.

And what about you? As you embark on the arduous journey of SEO mastery and business growth, as you learn from failures and celebrate the small victories, what fuels your relentless march forward?

Here's the inconvenient truth: if it doesn't matter to you, genuinely and profoundly, it won't matter to anyone else. Your customers, your readers, your audience—they all seek a connection with someone who's genuinely invested. They can sense when it's not there.

So I invite you to dig deep. Reflect on your life's narrative, the triumphs, and the tribulations. Unearth the moments that have led you to this juncture. Let them infuse your purpose with clarity and your persistence with meaning.

And remember, persistence is not about blind stubbornness. It's the delicate art of knowing when to pivot, when to persevere, and when to pause and reflect. It's about learning from every stumble and integrating those lessons into your next step forward.

As you continue to navigate through this book and apply its insights, let your 'why' be the lighthouse guiding you through the fog of uncertainty. Let it be the anchor that holds firm against the tides of challenge.

In the end, what matters to you will shape not only your actions but the legacy you leave. It's the difference between those who are remembered and those who are forgotten. It's the essence of true persistence.

Learning the Art of Persistence

YOUR PERSISTENT SELF

Within the expanse of your life, there are threads of persistence woven into the fabric of your daily existence. Everyone has them, areas where dedication doesn't waver, where commitment is as natural as breathing. It might be in the way you nurture relationships, maintain your health, or pursue hobbies with passion. Reflect for a moment on where you demonstrate persistence in your life. Is it in your unwavering dedication to family? The tenacity in learning a new skill? Or perhaps the sheer grit you show in facing life's adversities?

These reservoirs of persistence are testaments to your ability to commit, to pursue, to endure. They are also your greatest teachers. Understanding how you apply persistence in these areas can offer profound insights into how you can transfer this skill to other domains, like the formidable world of online marketing strategy.

Online marketing may not ignite your passion like your craft does. It's understandable. After all, you started your business to follow your love for what you do, not necessarily because you were thrilled by the idea of SEO, content marketing, or social media campaigns. Yet, in this digital age, your ability to share your craft with the world hinges on these very tools. This is where your persistent self needs to step forward.

It's time to approach online marketing with the same persistence you apply to other areas of your life. Begin by acknowledging that while you love your craft, the pathway to transforming it into a thriving business is paved with the bricks of marketing. Many business owners fall into the trap of outsourcing their marketing efforts entirely without grasping the basics themselves, only to find that without this understanding, they're at the mercy of others. And should they decide, they could compete against you with the knowledge they've acquired.

Therefore, becoming persistent in learning and applying online marketing principles is not just about business growth; it's about control, self-reliance, and truly owning the success of your enterprise. Think of it as learning the rules of a new game where the stakes are the future of your business. Dive into the strategy, the psychology of your audience, the analytics—equip yourself with the knowledge to understand what works and what doesn't, and why.

The persistence you've shown in other areas of life can be the blueprint. Break down the process of mastering online marketing into steps, as you would when tackling any complex task. Celebrate small victories to keep yourself motivated. Remember how you remained steadfast when things got tough in other pursuits and apply that resilience here.

Consider this: every blog post you write, every social media update you publish, every newsletter you send, is a thread in a larger tapestry that showcases your business to the world. It's a tapestry that can only be completed with a persistent hand and a strategic mind.

So, dear reader, embrace your persistent self. Look at your marketing hat not as an unwelcome necessity, but as a crown – one that you earn and reshape to fit the sovereign ruler of your destiny. Learn to market with the same persistence you live by, and watch as the world opens its doors to the craft you so dearly love to share.

TREASURE MAP MODE

TREASURE MAP MODE

Imagine for a moment that each month, you've been unknowingly subscribing to a game—a treasure hunt of sorts. It's a game you can play anytime, anywhere, though many remain unaware of its existence despite their monthly investment in it. This game? I like to call it the "Treasure Map Mode."

You see, life has endowed each one of us with a personal treasure map. Each day we breathe is an invitation to embark on a quest. It's your choice: you can either activate your map and engage with the world in a way that aligns with your desires, or you can keep it dormant.

Have you ever had a day where your thoughts seem to magnetically attract circumstances or opportunities? Perhaps it's a fleeting idea, and suddenly you find a hint, a breadcrumb, that pushes you in the right direction. This is not mere coincidence; this is "Treasure Map Mode" in action.

This mode is about heightened awareness. It's about synchronicity, where your internal world of thoughts and aspirations mirrors and affects your external reality. The more you tune in, the more you'll notice these breadcrumbs—hints that guide you closer to what you deeply yearn for.

Truth be told, I've been blessed to experience this magical mode multiple times. I'll be candid—it's something I wish I engaged with more often. This very book you're reading? It's a testament to those breadcrumbs I've followed. Despite my challenges with spelling and grammar, the universe has consistently presented me with the right people and resources to bring this dream to fruition.

Take, for instance, my friend and client, Kevin Levine from KTL Businesses. We were engaged in a spirited discussion about golf when Kevin was adamant he could match my shot distance. He had a multitude of reasons preventing him from doing so. However, when he opened himself up to some subtle tweaks I suggested, doors swung open for him. He was, without realizing it, on his own "Treasure Map Mode" journey.

Or consider the day I had the honor of interviewing Lee Stein on my podcast—a visionary credited with pioneering concepts in the world of email. That very morning, I had been pondering how wonderful it would be to have an intern to share the workload. As fate would have it, Lee, on his way to the interview, called to ask if he could bring along a friend looking for intern work. It was a eureka moment! That was when I first recognized the profound power of this "Treasure Map Mode."

More than ever, I'm convinced that whatever we focus on—be it sounds, sights, or feelings—it serves our future. It's our responsibility to piece these moments together, crafting a path to manifest our desires.

I urge you, dear reader, to be alert, be open, and embrace your journey. Activate your "Treasure Map Mode" and see where it leads. You might just find that everything you've ever wished for is waiting, hidden in plain sight.

Treasure Map Mode

TUNING INTO YOUR JOURNEY

Embarking on the Treasure Map Mode journey isn't just for life's big moments—it's applicable to every facet of life and business. To truly ascend as a "RankingMaster", I implore you to harness this latent power. The subscription to this game has been active since the day you were born, and you're paying for it with every heartbeat, every breath. So, why not make the most of it? As the saying goes, "tune in, tap on, and go."

Whenever you're ready, challenge yourself. Set a specific thought or goal into motion. What resonates with you almost immediately? What surprises await you around the corner? Remember, every twist and turn, even those that appear to lead you astray, could be guiding you to a back door—a detour offering essential tools or reshaping your path in unforeseen ways.

I'll be the first to admit: I haven't mastered this game. Just like you, I sometimes get lost in the mundane and stray from the path. That's the beauty and unpredictability of life. While some claim that it's possible to lead a 'perfect' life, I've yet to meet someone who truly embodies this ideal. But the Treasure Map Mode does allow us brief moments of perfection, sparks of pure synchronicity where everything falls into place.

Engage with this concept wholeheartedly. Dive in, practice regularly, and let playfulness guide you. The rewards you'll uncover are invaluable. And as you find your treasures, remember to share, inspire others, and always pay it forward.

Treasure Map Mode

TREASURE MAP MODE: IMMERSE AND EMBRACE

As you dive deeper into the pages of this book, I invite you to pause for a moment and activate your "Treasure Map Mode". Visualize it as the key that unlocks the full potential of "RankingMastery". Imagine this mode as a unique lens, allowing you to see beyond mere words and into the essence of the insights and wisdom that await.

By activating this mode, you're not just passively reading—you're actively seeking, connecting dots, and uncovering hidden treasures tailored for your journey. This mindset embeds "RankingMastery" into the very core of your being, making it an integral part of your DNA. It's like a beacon, guiding you toward the results and achievements you aspire to.

Approach each chapter with an open heart and a curious mind. Be receptive to the signs, hints, and nudges that resonate with your goals and aspirations. Remember, every breadcrumb you pick up and every connection you make leads you closer to mastering your rank in both the virtual and real worlds.

So, strap in and get ready for an enlightening ride. With your "Treasure Map Mode" activated and your senses heightened, you're not just reading—you're embarking on an adventure, with "RankingMastery" as your ultimate prize.

FAITH AND SUPER-NATURAL FAITH: A GUIDED EXPLORATION

SUPER-NATURAL FAITH: A GUIDED EXPLORATION

In "Super-Natural Faith: A Guided Exploration," we venture into the realm of an extraordinary force within us that transcends common understanding, a force that challenges the boundaries of our reality and broadens our horizons. This concept goes beyond mere luck or predetermined destiny; it's about nurturing a deep, unwavering faith that's almost super-natural in essence. But the question arises: how does one cultivate such a powerful faith and consistently let it guide their path?

To embark on this journey, one must first introspectively define what super-natural faith personally signifies. Is it an unwavering belief in oneself, an unshakeable trust in the cosmos, or a profound, divine connection that resonates within? Grasping the essence of what super-natural faith means to you is crucial in harnessing its transformative power.

Reflect on life's adversities and consider those moments of near-defeat, where an inner force propelled you forward against all odds. This resilience is the very seed of your super-natural faith. Contemplate how you can nurture this seed, ensuring its strength and presence in future challenges.

Cultivating such faith is an intentional act. It's about integrating daily practices that reinforce this belief system. Whether it's through affirmations, meditation, or absorbing motivational content, find what resonates with you and aligns with your vision of super-natural faith.

With this perspective, view your past challenges through a different lens and consider how you'll approach future obstacles. Instead of viewing them as barriers, can you perceive them as hidden opportunities for growth and enlightenment?

In the mundane routines of daily life, tactical strategies and connections have their importance, but super-natural faith operates on an entirely different spectrum. How can you ensure that your daily life doesn't overshadow this profound faith? What steps can you take to create a nurturing space for it to thrive and guide you?

The action plan is simple yet profound: start now. Dedicate time for introspection, jot down your interpretation of super-natural faith, and outline the initial steps towards cultivating it. Like any skill or mindset, it demands consistent practice and reinforcement.

Consider the incredible advancements of our age, such as the powerful, sleek smartphones that have become a routine part of our lives. These were once figments of imagination, deemed impossible. If such tangible innovations can materialize, then the boundless potential of super-natural faith is certainly within reach. The journey commences with a simple yet profound step, an introspective question: Are you ready to embrace and foster the super-natural faith within you?

Un Planned Lessons on Brand Ambassadorship

FROM BMX TO BRAND AMBASSADORSHIP

As I traveled the world, performing BMX stunts that left audiences in awe, I was living a reality that I hadn't fully grasped. Every twist in the air and every applause from the crowd was cementing my identity not just as a BMX professional, but as a symbol of what dedication to a craft could achieve.

At that time, the weight of being a brand ambassador for giants like GT, Pepsi, and Converse didn't fully dawn on me. It felt like another exciting chapter of my BMX journey, albeit with fancier shoes and the bubbly taste of cola. But as I think back, I realize the magnitude of it all. Here I was, a kid with a passion for BMX, suddenly representing brands with global recognition. These weren't just sponsorships; they were testaments to my skill and the potential they saw in aligning with my story.

The art of BMX was my language, but becoming a brand ambassador was like learning to communicate in a new dialect. It meant embodying the spirit of these brands, on and off the ramp.

It meant understanding that every jump or flip wasn't just for me or the audience but was also a reflection of these massive brands that had put their trust in me.

Looking back now, it's surreal. Being thrust into such roles was similar to a masterclass in branding, marketing, and influence. I was living an experience that many entrepreneurs dream of. And now, as I delve into the business world, I realize the goldmine of experiences I've amassed. Every handshake, every crowd's cheer, every brand endorsement wasn't just a fleeting moment; it was a lesson, a stepping stone.

Today, as I navigate the world of entrepreneurship, these memories aren't just nostalgic remnants of my past. They're invaluable assets, unparalleled experiences that give me an edge. To start a business with such a rich history, with stories that can captivate audiences and foster connections, is a privilege. It's a realization that my BMX days weren't just about thrill and adrenaline; they were unknowingly grooming me for the business world, teaching me about branding, influence, and the power of a compelling story.

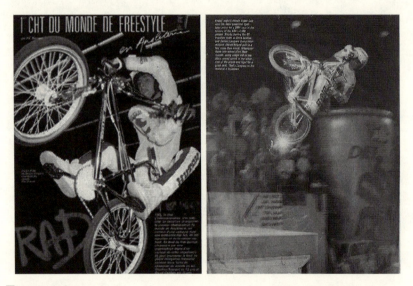

Figure 1.9:

MASTERING THE FUNDAMENTALS OF SEO WEBPAGE STRUCTURE

SEO STRATEGY APPLIES TO EVERYTHING ONLINE

In today's digital landscape, understanding and applying the fundamental elements of SEO is no longer a mere option but a necessity for anyone keen on capturing online visibility and success. Whether you're drafting a blog post, constructing your website, or even sharing content on platforms like Facebook or Instagram, incorporating key SEO principles can significantly amplify your reach. Consider your Page Title or a social media post title; it's the first interaction potential clients have with your content. A compelling, keyword-rich title can pique interest and drastically increase click-through rates. Similarly, a well-crafted Meta Description or post caption can provide just enough intrigue to pull readers from their online browsing into your content.

Now, let's dive into the URL Structure, similar to the usernames or page URLs you select on social platforms. A clean, straightforward URL that reflects your brand or content can enhance memorability and trustworthiness. Moving on to your content's body, whether it's a detailed service description on your website or a concise Instagram post, structured, keyword-conscious content is crucial. It should inform, engage, and call your audience to action. Utilizing Heading Tags in your blogs, like using bold or capitalized text in your social media posts, helps break down content into digestible, attention-grabbing sections.

The practice of linking, too, is universal. On your website, Internal and External Links boost your SEO strength and provide additional value to your readers, similar to sharing links in your social media bios or posts, guiding your followers to your newest product or a valued partner's platform. And let's not forget the power of visuals; optimizing Images with Alt Text on your site ensures search engines can 'see' your images. In contrast, using high-quality, relevant images on social media is an absolute must-do to grab attention.

Here's a relatable example: Imagine you're a health coach posting on Instagram. Your username (URL Structure) could be @JohnDoeHealthCoach, clear and memorable. The post's title, possibly your image's first text or caption, could be "5 Energy-Boosting Foods for Fall" (Page Title), with a captivating image of the foods you're discussing (Images). Your caption (Meta Description) could start with a compelling question or statement, then briefly explain what you'll be discussing, using relevant hashtags (keywords) like #HealthCoachTips. You might then have a link in your bio (Internal Link) to your latest blog post on the same topic, extending your audience's journey with your content.

In essence, mastering these SEO fundamentals and adapting them across all your digital content isn't just a strategy; it's the backbone of your online presence. When done right, it connects you to your audience in a meaningful, memorable, and actionable way, setting the stage for sustained growth and success.

MASTERING THE FUNDAMENTALS OF SEO WEBPAGE STRUCTURE

FUNDAMENTALS OF SEO WEBPAGE STRUCTURE

1. Introduction: The Power of SEO

Start with an analogy or a story that emphasizes the importance of SEO. Highlight how an optimized page can drive traffic, boost sales, and increase brand visibility.

2. Page Title (Title Tag)

- Definition: Briefly explain that the title tag is the clickable headline that appears in search engine results.
- Importance: It provides users and search engines an insight into the content topic.

Tips:
- Be concise and descriptive.
- Include your primary keyword towards the beginning.

- Keep it within 50-60 characters to ensure it displays correctly in search results.

3. Meta Description

- Definition: A brief summary (around 155 characters) of a page's content.
- Importance: It can influence click-through rates by providing a concise summary to potential visitors.

Tips:
- Ensure it's compelling and descriptive.
- Include your primary keyword.
- Make it action-oriented.

4. URL Structure

- Definition: The web address of your page.
- Importance: A clear URL can provide both users and search engines an idea of the page topic.

Tips:
- Keep it short and descriptive.
- Use hyphens to separate words.
- Include the main keyword.

5. Heading Tags (H1, H2, H3,...)

- Definition: HTML tags used for distinguishing headings and subheadings within content.
- Importance: They provide structure and context to your content and help search engines understand the hierarchy.

Tips:

- Only use one H1 tag per page (typically the page's title).
- Use H2s for main headings, H3s for subheadings, and so on.
- Incorporate relevant keywords without keyword stuffing.

6. Page Content

- Definition: The main body of your webpage.
- Importance: Quality content answers users' questions, establishes your expertise, and engages your audience.

Tips:
- Create unique and high-quality content.
- Ensure content is structured, easy to read, and divided into sections with headings.
- Naturally integrate keywords and related terms.

7. Internal and External Links

- Definition: Hyperlinks that point to related content within your website (internal) or to other websites (external).
- Importance: They help establish content hierarchy, spread page authority, and provide further reading opportunities.

Tips:
- Use descriptive anchor text.
- Link to reputable external sources.
- Ensure internal links point to relevant and related content.

8. Images and Alt Text

- Definition: Visual elements on your page and the descriptive text that explains the image (if it doesn't load or for screen readers).
- Importance: Images enhance user experience, while alt text ensures accessibility and helps search engines understand the image content.

Tips:
- Use high-quality images relevant to your content.
- Keep file sizes optimized to ensure quick loading.
- Always include descriptive alt text, incorporating keywords where relevant.

9. The Integrated Webpage

Wrap up by emphasizing the importance of integrating all these elements. When combined, these fundamental components can work harmoniously to boost a page's SEO while providing valuable content for readers.

Throughout the chapter, use simple language, clear examples, and practical tips. Aim to demystify SEO, making it accessible and actionable for your readers.

SOCIETAL HIERARCHIES AND MORE HANDS

SOCIETAL HIERARCHIES AND MORE HANDS: THE DIGITAL PARALLEL

In our day-to-day lives, we all know, or at least have heard of, someone who seems to be incredibly "connected." They're the ones who seem to have a friend or an acquaintance in every influential circle. Whether it's the chief of police, the manager of the poshest restaurant in town, or close connections with professional sports players - these individuals possess an impressive Rolodex. Their phone call is an invite to that newly opened restaurant where reservations seem almost impossible. They casually offer tickets to events, like the Super Bowl, where most people would pay thousands just to be present. It's all about the connections, the networks they've woven, and the societal hierarchies they've adeptly navigated.

In the vast realm of the internet, websites also exist within a similar structure of hierarchies. And just like in the real world, who you know or, in the digital sphere, who links to you, makes all the difference.

Consider this: You run a computer repair shop specializing in Apple products. Now, imagine Apple themselves recommending your services on their platform, providing a direct link to your site. This nod of approval doesn't just boost your credibility; it propels your online status. Apple, a titan in the digital domain, exists at one of the highest tiers of online hierarchies. Their acknowledgment, their "digital handshake" if you will, is similar to receiving an invite from that ultra-connected individual in real life.

Search engines, the gatekeepers of the internet, recognize these digital handshakes. When a renowned entity points in your direction, it's an endorsement, an assurance of your quality and reliability. It's like being "invited to the game" by someone from the highest echelons of society. You're given a seat at the table.

In my own journey, I've realized the sheer power of being associated with high-traffic platforms. My podcast and YouTube channel, for instance, have served as pivotal connectors in this digital web. These platforms, brimming with audience engagement and authority, have not just amplified my voice but have significantly boosted my online rank. Every feature, every mention, every backlink from these platforms was like a gold coin added to my digital treasure chest. The more affluent and authoritative the source, the richer my digital worth became.

But remember, it's not just about chasing high-traffic platforms. It's about creating value, being genuine, and fostering genuine connections in the digital realm. Just as in real life, genuine relationships and authentic endorsements always triumph.

So, as you venture into the digital world, keep in mind the societal hierarchies and the power of connections. Aim to be that person, that website, which isn't just well-ranked but well-respected. For in the world of "Ranking Mastery", these two often go hand in hand.

Societal Hierarchies and More Hands

WIN-WIN RANKING IN SEARCH IS MONEY TODAY AND TOMORROW

Imagine for a moment you own a piece of land. It's not just any land; it's a plot situated on a commonly traversed route between San Diego and Las Vegas. At first, this piece of real estate may not seem like much. You watch countless cars pass by, each of them likely unaware of the potential that this patch of earth holds. Over the years, I've journeyed on this very route, witnessing firsthand its transformation.

Just over the Nevada border, there was a modest gas station. The sole oasis in a long stretch of highway, it became an essential pitstop for travelers wary of running on empty before reaching Las Vegas. Over time, this gas station didn't just offer fuel but became a beacon, signaling the last point of rest before the final dash to the city.

As years rolled by, the landscape began to change. Another entrepreneur, seeing the steady traffic at the first gas station, decided to set up shop on the opposite side of the highway. And then, as if overnight, a significant investor saw potential in this small but bustling stopover. The desert land transformed with the establishment of a grand casino.

Now, imagine the value surge for that first gas station. What was once a humble pitstop now found itself in the midst of a thriving commercial hub. Its plot's worth skyrocketed, much like a diamond suddenly discovered in a long-overlooked mine.

This story mirrors the world of digital real estate. Your website, similar to that piece of land, holds incredible potential value. With time, effort, and strategic positioning, especially in high-traffic keyword arenas, your digital property doesn't just enhance visibility or business prospects; it adds significant weight to your net worth.

When I reflect upon my journey with "Perfection on Wheels", I'm reminded of this very principle. The valuation of the business was profoundly influenced by our digital assets. While tangible equipment depreciated over time, our well-ranking websites appreciated in value, standing as testimonies to the power of digital ranking. They weren't just platforms for business; they were assets, steadily increasing in worth with each passing day.

In essence, your website's rank on search engines is similar to owning prime real estate in a burgeoning neighborhood. With careful cultivation and investment, it matures from just a plot of digital land to a property that appreciates over time. Every effort you invest in ensuring your website ranks high in search results translates not just into immediate business benefits but in increasing the overall value of your business for future gains.

So, as you ponder on investments and assets, think digital. In today's world, a high-ranking website isn't just about immediate traffic; it's about laying the foundation for a prosperous future. Like that gas station en route to Las Vegas, you too can find your website transformed from a simple platform into a hub of opportunity and value.

Societal Hierarchies and More Hands

MORE HANDS IN THE ROOM

Imagine being in a grand, chandelier-lit ballroom. At the front stands a renowned speaker, someone you've long admired. This individual possesses the key to unlocking your business's next phase of growth, and all you wish for is a sliver of their attention. As they scan the room, ready to answer a question, you raise your hand, hoping against hope that you'll be the chosen one.

But then, a thought crosses your mind: What if you could stack the odds in your favor?

Visualize that instead of just your lone hand, there are dozens, all reaching up with the same urgency, the same question. You've cleverly spread out friends or teammates across the room, and they're all waiting, hoping to be chosen. Their synchronized effort makes it almost impossible for the speaker to ignore your collective presence. That's the power of numbers.

This analogy perfectly encapsulates the strategy I deployed in the vast world of Google search. By creating multiple websites and videos targeting specific keyword phrases, I was essentially increasing my 'hands in the room', drawing Google's attention repeatedly to my content. With each site and video, I was optimizing, refining, ensuring it was drenched with relevance to those specific keywords. The outcome? My content started to dominate the search results, grabbing not just one, but multiple top-ranking spots.

The result was nothing short of magical: owning 4 out of the top 10 spots in a Google search. Think about that! With every search, I had a 40% chance of being the go-to choice. It was as if, in a room of ten people, four were vying on my behalf, waving their hands, and clamoring for attention.

The lesson here is clear: in the vast digital realm, where attention is gold, having 'more hands in the room' by spreading your content across multiple platforms and sites can amplify your presence, enhance your visibility, and ultimately lead to more clients, more trust, and yes, more revenue.

And this isn't just a strategy; it's a philosophy. It's about recognizing that in today's digital age, quantity, when combined with quality, can be a game-changer. So, ask yourself: How many 'hands' do you currently have in the room, and how can you increase that number to maximize your chances?

THE "AVATAR"

CRAFTING YOUR SIGNATURE AVATAR: THE ART OF MEMORABLE BRANDING

Picture a black turtleneck, and Steve Jobs springs to mind. A grey T-shirt? That's Mark Zuckerberg. A signature red tie is unmistakably Donald Trump. And a Nike golf shirt? You're likely envisioning Tiger Woods, striding confidently across the green. These are more than just pieces of clothing; they're powerful visual elements that constitute these individuals' personal avatars. These icons have crafted an enduring, memorable visual identity through their consistent sartorial choices, and so can you.

Your personal avatar is more than just your preferred style of dress; it's a strategic tool that, when used effectively, can anchor your personal and professional brand in the minds of others. But how does one go about creating a signature style that's both authentic and memorable? Let's delve into this artful strategy.

1. The Self-Reflection Process:
Creating your avatar begins with introspection. What makes you feel most confident? Most authentic? This could be a certain color that you believe brings out the best in you, a specific style

that resonates with your personality, or even an accessory that holds significant meaning. This process is about identifying your essence and how best to visually express it.

2. Consistency is Key:
The power of a personal avatar comes from consistency. It's about choosing a signature element and sticking with it, whether you're attending a casual event, speaking at a conference, or posting on social media. This repetitive visual cue becomes synonymous with your brand.

3. Balancing Comfort and Statement:
While your avatar should make a statement, it shouldn't come at the cost of your comfort. Choose something that you can confidently carry because genuine comfort radiates a natural confidence that's integral to brand authenticity.

4. The Evolution of an Avatar:
Even the most iconic avatars can evolve over time. However, any changes should be gradual and strategic, never straying too far from the core visual identity that people recognize and associate with you.

5. Beyond Clothing:
An avatar isn't limited to apparel. It encompasses your overall presentation, including your hairstyle, any accessories, a distinct tone of voice, or even a catchphrase you regularly use. All these elements come together to create a comprehensive, memorable persona.

6. Avatar and Business Branding:

Integrating your personal avatar with your business branding creates a powerful, unified message. For instance, if your avatar includes a relaxed beach vibe, that can translate into your professional realm, perhaps through your business's branding visuals, mission statement, or work culture.

7. The Universal Recognition:

Imagine the power of being recognized by a simple item of clothing or style. A Nike golf shirt isn't just a piece of apparel; it's Tiger Woods on the final hole at the Masters. Your avatar can have the same instant recognition, associated with your values, achievements, and the essence of who you are.

In conclusion, your signature avatar is a visual representation of your personal and professional identity. It's an influential tool that, when crafted mindfully and worn consistently, can stand the test of time. As you forge your path, consider the visual legacy you wish to create. How will the world remember you? What will be your black turtleneck, your grey T-shirt, your Nike golf shirt? The creation of your avatar is more than a sartorial choice; it's a strategic decision that can resonate for years to come.

TRADITIONAL WEBSITES, SALES FUNNELS, SEO LANDING PAGES

THE WEBSITE

In the digital marketplace of today, the concept of a website has evolved significantly. If we draw parallels with the medical field, what once was a general practitioner handling a plethora of tasks has now morphed into a host of specialists, each with their unique expertise and purpose. The website is no different.

Originally, a website was similar to a digital storefront or business card, a one-size-fits-all solution where a company or individual could showcase their offerings to the world. Now, just as doctors have honed their skills to specialize in cardiology, orthopedics, or ophthalmology, websites too have transformed to serve very particular roles in the pursuit of a specific goal.

Today's website can still serve as a digital brochure, but this is just the tip of the iceberg. Below the surface, there are several specialized forms of web presence, each crafted to meet diverse strategic objectives. Here are a few examples:

The Brochure Website:

Think of this as your online leaflet. A brochure website is the simplest form of a website, designed primarily for informational purposes. It's the digital equivalent of a physical brochure you might pick up to learn about a company's products or services. With a focus on providing visitors with essential information about the business, its values, and contacts, this type of website is perfect for small businesses, consultants, or professionals looking to establish an online presence without requiring advanced functionality.

The Sales Funnel:

Imagine a guide leading a customer through a journey. A sales funnel isn't just a website; it's a carefully crafted path designed to convert visitors into customers. Each page, each piece of content, and every call to action is strategically placed to guide potential customers towards making a purchase. From the awareness stage, through consideration, and finally to the decision, a sales funnel narrows down prospects at each step, ensuring that only those with genuine interest make it through to your final call to action, be it a purchase, a subscription, or another form of conversion.

The SEO Landing Page:
Consider this the specialist among general practitioners. An SEO landing page is created with a laser-focused intent of ranking for a specific keyword or phrase in search engine results. It's highly optimized for search engines with the goal of drawing

in organic traffic from searches relevant to the content on the page. The content is often structured to not only be SEO-friendly but to also provide value to the reader, answering specific questions, or offering solutions to their search queries. The objective of an SEO landing page is to rank highly, draw in targeted traffic, and convert that traffic based on the page's specific goals, which could be anything from lead generation to direct sales.

Each type of website uses distinct design elements, content strategies, and user experience optimizations to fulfill its specific purpose. As we move on to talk about funnels and SEO landing pages, remember that just like a specialist doctor, each of these website types requires a deep understanding of its unique function and audience to be effective.

In the upcoming sections, we'll dissect and discuss each type of specialized web page in detail. We'll explore how a funnel is tailored to guide a customer through the buying process, and how SEO landing pages are designed with precision to target specific keywords and achieve organic visibility. Understanding these specialized web entities is crucial for anyone looking to establish a dominant online presence.

THE BLEND OF SEO KEY PHRASES WITH SALES

THE ART OF CONTENT ALCHEMY: TURNING KEYWORDS INTO GOLD WITH SALES-INFUSED SEO

In the digital age, content is the line we cast into the vast ocean of the internet, hoping to hook customers. But not all content is created equal. Some are like feeble twigs, easily ignored by the swimmers below. Others? They're golden lures, irresistible and promising, drawing in a bounty of clients eager to bite. The secret? A masterful blend of sales language and SEO-rich content that serves as both bait and beacon. In this chapter, we delve into the art of creating content that doesn't just attract but persuades and converts

.

First, understand your foundation: the keywords. These aren't merely SEO tools; they're whispers of your customer's desires, needs, and curiosities. Your first task is to listen closely. What solutions are your potential clients seeking? What language do they use, and what intent lurks behind their queries? This understanding is the bedrock upon which you'll build your content.

Now, enter the realm of sales psychology. Your content shouldn't scream promotion; that's the quickest way to send your audience scurrying away. Instead, it should resonate with empathy, echo with authority, and shine with the promise of resolution. You're not just selling a product or service; you're presenting a key to unlock better versions of their personal or professional lives. And this key, subtly woven into your content, opens not just their wallets, but their trust.

But how do you merge SEO with persuasive narrative seamlessly? Here's the golden rule: your keywords are important, but they're the threads, not the tapestry. They should be so organically interwoven that your reader is guided gently down a path of convincing, relatable storytelling that just happens to lead to your solution. Overstuffing your content with keywords is similar to a sea with too many lures; it confuses and overwhelms the swimmer, and they'll likely swim away.

Let's break down the anatomy of golden content:

1. Empathetic Understanding: Start by addressing a pain point or aspiration you know resonates with your

audience, based on your keyword research. Show them you understand, you care, and you've been listening.

2. Educational Value: Provide them with insightful information or a fresh perspective they hadn't considered. This positions you as an authority and builds trust.

3. Seamless Integration: Sprinkle keywords naturally throughout, using them to reinforce your narrative rather than define it. They should flow within your content, not stick out awkwardly.

4. The Art of the Story: Everyone loves a good story. Whether it's a client testimonial, a success story, or your own journey, a well-told narrative can be a powerful sales tool.

5. Call to Action (CTA): This isn't just a button or a closing sentence. It's a climactic promise, an irresistible invitation for a grander adventure. Craft it with care, excitement, and anticipation.

Remember, the internet is an ocean teeming with fish, all seeking something. If you cast the right content—strategically designed, empathetically written, and SEO-enhanced—you're not just fishing; you're calling to the sea, promising bounty and a safe harbor.

So, entrepreneur, ready your ships. It's time to set sail and venture into the waters of content alchemy, where your words are the lures, your understanding is the hook, and your offerings are the treasure yet unclaimed.

THE BLEND OF SEO KEY PHRASES WITH SALES

RANKING BEFORE SALES

In the world of digital marketing, the adage "walk before you run" takes on a particular significance. Many entrepreneurs, eager to see immediate returns, leap straight into sales-focused strategies. Yet, before a sale can ever happen, there's a crucial step that must not be overlooked: ranking. Your website's visibility on search engines is the foundation upon which sales are built. It's about ensuring that your site is the one people find when they're searching for the solutions you offer.

The priority, especially when you're starting out or launching a new product, has to be on mastering SEO. It's about getting your pages to climb the ranks of Google's search results for relevant queries. This focus on SEO isn't just about playing the long game; it's about building the infrastructure that will support and sustain sales in the future.

Of course, this doesn't mean your pages should be devoid of sales elements. On the contrary, they should be designed to convert visitors into leads and customers. But the art lies in finding the right balance. It's about creating content that is relevant and valuable, content that will bring your pages to the forefront of search results. Once you've achieved visibility and you're ranking well, that's when the sales elements can take a more prominent role.

Think of SEO as the stage on which your sales performance will take place. First, you build the stage, make sure it's solid, and position it where the audience can see it. Only then do you step into the spotlight and start your sales pitch. The approach we advocate in our software products mirrors this philosophy. We ensure that the focus on SEO and content relevance is strong so that when it's time to introduce sales elements, they're performing to an already captivated audience.

If you're new to the SEO game or haven't had much success in getting ranked, let's start with the basics. Focus on creating content that's rich in the keywords and phrases your potential customers are searching for. Make it valuable, make it authoritative, and make sure it's the answer to the queries being posed. This is your 'walk' before the 'run' of sales. Once you've mastered this, you've laid the groundwork for a sales strategy that has the visibility to truly shine.

CREATING YOUR FIRST WEBSITE LANDING PAGES

THE UNSEEN GOLDMINE: INVESTING TIME IN YOUR ONLINE REAL ESTATE

Imagine you're in a vast hall, a seminar that holds the answers to your business's growth, success, and maybe even survival. But you're not just one in the crowd; you're lost in a sea of faces, all eager for the same lifeline, the same attention from the guest speaker you're desperate to connect with. What do you do? You don't just sit there, hoping against hope. No, you bring in reinforcements. You scatter your friends across the room, increasing your chances of being seen, of being heard, of connecting. That's precisely what building individual pages on your website is like. It's not just about creating a single point of contact but about spreading out, occupying as much space as you can to increase the likelihood of connecting with your audience, your customers.

Now, I know what you're thinking. Creating these pages is laborious, time-consuming, and frankly, not the most exciting part of your business journey. But here's where I want you to shift your perspective. These pages, once created and optimized, don't just exist for a day, a week, or even a year. They stand as a testament to your business, your brand, for eternity in the digital world. They continue to connect, continue to bring in leads, continue to generate revenue without any additional effort.

Take, for instance, my experience with "Perfection On Wheels." Years ago, we created a simple, unassuming page targeting "Red Ribbon Week School Assemblies." It wasn't a marvel of design, far from it, but it was functional, and it served a specific purpose. You might stumble upon it even now, and it stands as a prime example of digital endurance. Since its inception in 2007, I can conservatively attribute leads that have generated sales of at least 2 million dollars to this single, basic page. That's the power of creating something and letting it live in the online space.\

But remember, the pages you procrastinate on, the pages you decide not to create, can't yield anything. They don't exist, and what doesn't exist has zero chance of generating leads or sales. It's like not asking your question at the seminar at all. Silence leads to invisibility, and invisibility can't bring growth.

So, as you sit there, contemplating the effort versus the reward, I want you to think not of the hours you'll spend crafting these pages but of the years they'll spend working for you. Your goal, the reason you're turning these pages, is to elevate your online presence and, in turn, increase your revenue. Each page you create is not just a shot at achieving this but a step closer to the success you envision. And the beautiful part? Once done, they continue to work for you, tirelessly, ceaselessly, perpetually.

In simple terms, think of every web page as a lottery ticket. Sure, it takes effort to go and buy one, but without that ticket, you have no chance to win. However, with each ticket, with each new page, you're increasing your odds exponentially. And the best part? These 'lottery tickets' don't expire; they keep on giving you a chance to win, year after year. So, roll up your sleeves and start creating; your future self, reaping the rewards, will thank you for it.

Creating Your First Website Landing Pages

WHAT WOULD YOU DO WITH AN EXTRA $4600?

Chapter: The Path to Massive Savings: Would You Walk It?

Have you ever found yourself staring at a task so vast and time-consuming, you couldn't fathom how you'd tackle it efficiently? Imagine you're on the brink of a project that's estimated to eat up 160 hours of your time.

How would you feel if you could accomplish that in a fraction of the estimated duration? How much is your time worth? Let's say you value it conservatively at $30 an hour. If you could save, hypothetically, 154 of those 160 hours, that's a savings of $4,620.

What could you do with that extra time and money?

- Take a vacation?

- Invest in another project?

- Or perhaps scale your business further?

Now, let me pose another question: if there was a tool that promised to deliver these time savings, would you be skeptical? It's only natural. There's no shortage of tools and platforms making bold claims about revolutionizing processes, but how many live up to the hype?

But what if I told you that such a tool doesn't just exist, but has already been proven with businesses just like yours? Would that pique your curiosity?

ENTER RANKINGMASTERY

It transformed the daunting task faced by KTL Business Insurance of generating 84 SEO-optimized pages from a 160-hour endeavor into a swift 6-hour task. That's not merely efficiency; it's groundbreaking.

You might wonder: What's the secret sauce? Is it user-friendly? Does it have integrated SEO tools? Is there a template system to streamline the process? The answer to all these questions is a resounding yes.

But beyond the features and benefits, here's the crux: In a digital age where efficiency and agility define business success, can you afford not to have a tool like RankingMastery in your arsenal?

So, circling back to the initial premise: If you had a pathway to save 154 hours and over $4,600, would you walk it? With RankingMastery, you're not just investing in a tool; you're investing in a future where you work smarter, not harder. Are you ready to step into that future?

Creating Your First Website Landing Pages

EMBRACING A PHILOSOPHY

With RankingMastery, you're not just investing in a tool; you're embracing a philosophy. This isn't merely about automating mundane tasks or cutting down on hours spent behind a screen; it's about fundamentally reimagining how you approach your online presence. You're positioning yourself in a realm where technology empowers creativity, where the hours saved spell opportunities for innovation, strategy, and personal growth.

Consider this: each hour saved is an hour earned, a currency you can spend on brainstorming your next big venture, forging deeper connections with your clientele, or even enhancing your work-life balance. This isn't just a time-saver; it's a life enhancer.

However, embracing RankingMastery isn't an end—it's a significant leap forward, a step towards a future where your business doesn't just survive but thrives. The digital landscape is vast and ever-evolving, and while this tool is your compass, the journey doesn't end here.

As we navigate the complexities of the online world, our work together continues. There are strategies to refine, innovations to harness, and successes to chase. And while RankingMastery can be a linchpin in your digital strategy, it takes a visionary like you to truly exploit its potential.

Now, you have the chance to integrate this powerful software into your strategy. You can sign up, become part of the RankingMastery community, and start experiencing the transformative effects of efficiency combined with strategic acumen.

But remember, we're in this together, and this step, as monumental as it is, is part of a larger journey. A journey of adaptation, of learning, of growth. It's the journey of a forward-thinker who is not content with the status quo but is always reaching for the extraordinary.

Are you ready to step into this future, with all its potential and promise? The tools are here, the door is open, and the opportunity is yours for the taking. But rest assured, this is a journey we are committed to walking alongside you. The adventure is far from over; in many ways, it's just beginning.

Creating Your First Website Landing Pages

FROM FACE-TO-FACE TO DIGITAL MARKETING

From Face-to-Face to Click-to-Click: Adapting Your Marketing Mindset for the Digital Era

In the digital age, transitioning from traditional, face-to-face marketing to online marketing can be a challenging shift. It requires a recalibration of strategies and tactics, but at its core, it still leans heavily on the principles of understanding, connecting, and serving your audience. Here's how you can adapt your mindset for online success:

1. Empathy Still Reigns Supreme

Whether in a physical store or on a website, the foundation of effective marketing is understanding your customer. Online, you may not see their facial expressions or hear the tone of their voice, but by analyzing user behavior, comments, and feedback, you can still tune into their emotions and needs.

2. Crafting a Digital Persona

In face-to-face marketing, you might have relied on your charisma, voice modulation, or physical cues to engage a potential client. Online, these elements translate into website design, content tone, and user experience. Your website becomes your digital storefront and spokesperson. Make sure it embodies the best qualities of your brand.

3. Addressing Virtual Pain Points

In person, you might have directly asked a customer about their needs or concerns. On the web, you need to anticipate these pain points based on keyword research, online queries, and common industry issues. Address these proactively in your content to position yourself as a go-to solution provider.

4. Engagement Beyond Physical Presence

You can't shake hands or make direct eye contact online, but you can still engage. Use tools like live chat, comments sections, or even interactive quizzes and polls to create dynamic interactions. Respond promptly and genuinely to build trust.

5. Staying Updated with Digital Trends

Just as you might have adjusted your in-person approach based on societal or local trends, online marketing requires staying updated with digital trends. Whether it's a new social media platform, a change in search engine algorithms, or emerging web technologies, be prepared to adapt and evolve.

In summary, while the mediums have changed, the underlying principles of marketing remain rooted in genuine human connection. By understanding this and adapting your strategies accordingly, you can seamlessly transition from traditional to digital marketing, ensuring you connect meaningfully with your audience, no matter the platform.

MINING KEYWORDS: UNEARTH THE PHRASES YOUR CUSTOMERS ARE SEARCHING FOR

Imagine the world's information at your fingertips, and each query you type into that familiar search bar is a direct line to understanding your customer's thoughts, needs, and desires. This isn't a futuristic fantasy; this is the power of keyword research in today's digital marketing landscape. And the beauty of it? You don't need to be a marketing guru to start reaping its benefits.

Start simple. Open Google, and begin typing phrases relevant to your business. Pay attention to the suggested searches that auto-populate. These aren't random words; they're reflections of the most frequent queries from users across the globe, effectively giving you a sneak peek into the collective mind of your consumer base. Jot these down, even if they don't seem entirely relevant at first glance. What you're building is a reservoir of potential; these are the streams of curiosity you can tap into.

Now, let's shrink our focus but deepen our insight. Head over to YouTube and enter those same phrases. What pops up? Videos, and lots of them. But don't just look at the titles; look at the view counts. These aren't just videos; they're proof of interest, engagement, and demand. Each view represents a potential customer, someone who sought out content based on the very keywords you listed.

But here's the kicker: this could be you. Each of those videos could be showcasing your product, your service, your brand. Those views could be clicks onto your website, calls to your office, sales in your ledger. All because you understood what your customers were looking for and positioned yourself as the answer.

Remember, Google isn't just a search engine; it's a signal station broadcasting the needs and wants of millions. It's inviting businesses—inviting you—to step up and respond. And when you do, it's not just answering a query; it's beginning a conversation, making a connection, and establishing a relationship.

So keep building that keyword list, because those words are more than terms on a screen; they're opportunities knocking on your digital door. Will you answer?

BEYOND THE SEARCH BAR: LEVERAGING HIDDEN OPPORTUNITIES IN YOUR KEYWORD TREASURE TROVE

Every entrepreneur dreams of striking gold in their business, but what if I told you that the golden nuggets are already in your possession, just waiting to be unearthed and capitalized on? This isn't about inventing a new product or pivoting your business model; it's about seeing the familiar landscape of your business through the fresh, revealing lens of keyword research.

Once you have that comprehensive list of keywords and phrases, the real fun begins. Scrutinize this list; it's more than a collection of popular search terms. It's a direct transcript of your potential customers' needs, questions, and, most crucially, opportunities.

Identify the terms that resonate with your business's core competencies, but don't stop there. Be on the lookout for questions your customers are asking, the ones you know your business can answer. These queries are conversational entry points, and responding to them doesn't just promote your product; it establishes you as an authority in your field.

Now, let's talk about the unexpected windfalls. Throughout my entrepreneurial journey, I've repeatedly discovered that assets I'd sidelined or underestimated were, in fact, hidden treasure chests. It all started with my BMX business. Our half-pipe ramps, colossal and costly, were used primarily for county fairs or corporate events. However, a curious trend in keyword searches revealed an untapped market: Hollywood. These ramps, idle between shows, were suddenly in demand as backdrops in commercials and movies, commanding rates we hadn't imagined.

So, what's your "half-pipe ramp"? Maybe you own intellectual property that could be educational content for an online course. Perhaps your quaint bed-and-breakfast can serve as a rustic wedding venue in the off-season. Or your team's digital marketing expertise can be packaged into a webinar series. The possibilities are as varied as the businesses reading this book.

Here's a task: look around your business. Consider your assets, physical and intangible. Now, return to your keyword list. Are there search terms or questions that shed new light on these assets? Is there a way they can address a need, answer a question, or solve a problem in a context you hadn't considered before?

This exercise isn't a one-off event; it's a habit. The market evolves, trends shift, and new opportunities emerge. Regularly revisiting your keyword research keeps your business dynamic, relevant, and, above all, profitable in ways you hadn't foreseen.

Remember, the opportunities aren't just in the search results; they're in interpreting them with a creative, strategic, and open-minded view. And sometimes, they're hiding in plain sight, within the assets you already own.

From Face-to-Face to Digital Marketing

SAMPLES OF CREATING SEO SALES CONTENT FOR YOUR WEBPAGE

SAMPLE 1: DENTIST IN SAN DIEGO

Before SEO and Sales Infusion:

"Our dental clinic offers a range of services from teeth cleaning to dental implants. Our experienced staff ensures that you have a comfortable visit every time."

After SEO and Sales Infusion:

"Looking for a San Diego dentist who truly understands your needs? Dive into a transformative dental experience right in the heart of San Diego, where your smile's health and radiance is our passion. From gentle teeth cleaning sessions to state-of-the-art dental implants, our dedicated team ensures not just impeccable results but a journey that feels like home."

SAMPLE 2: ORGANIC TEA E-COMMERCE STORE

Before SEO and Sales Infusion:

"We sell organic teas sourced from the best gardens. Our collection boasts a variety of flavors."

After SEO and Sales Infusion:

"Awaken your senses with our enchanting range of organic teas. Handpicked from the world's pristine gardens, every sip promises an authentic embrace of nature's finest flavors. Whether you're a green tea enthusiast or an herbal blend lover, our curated collection invites you to a voyage of exquisite taste, all from the comfort of your home."

Sample 3: Online Fitness Training Platform

Before SEO and Sales Infusion:

"We offer online fitness classes with certified trainers. Join us to achieve your fitness goals."

After SEO and Sales Infusion:

"Embark on a transformative online fitness journey tailored just for you. With our certified trainers at your side, every squat, lift, and stretch is a step closer to your ultimate fitness dream. Dive into dynamic sessions, harness cutting-edge advice, and watch as your goals evolve from aspirations to achievements."

Sample 4: Digital Marketing Agency

Before SEO and Sales Infusion:

"We provide digital marketing services to boost your online presence."

After SEO and Sales Infusion:

"Ready to dominate the digital realm? Our digital marketing maestros craft bespoke strategies that elevate your brand's online footprint, turning browsers into believers and clicks into loyal customers. Unveil the power of tailored marketing, and watch as the digital world becomes your playground."

Each sample demonstrates a seamless integration of keywords while maintaining a persuasive narrative. The goal is to resonate with the reader emotionally while also satisfying the SEO requirements.

THE CAUSE OF ACCOMPLISHMENT

THE QUEST FOR SIGNIFICANCE

The ebb and flow of this narrative, oscillating between strategies for digital "Ranking" and the pursuit of personal excellence, underscores a fundamental truth: life, both online and offline, is governed by similar dynamics. To some, the parallels might seem evident and actionable. Those are the ones with an innate drive, a pre-configured DNA that compels them to seize upon insights and turn them into realities. Yet, there are others who meander, their gazes wandering, ever susceptible to the glitter of new distractions. And truly, who can fault them? In an age of relentless information and endless options, the temptation to leap from one shiny prospect to the next is all too real.

Often, in moments of reflection, I see my own journey mirrored in these narratives. Torn between the need to stay fit and play golf, and the inexorable pull of this book and software project, I too grapple with conflicting demands. And as these words spill onto the page, a poignant memory resurfaces: that childhood 'switch' when the concept of "real time simulation of winning or accomplishing" took root within me. It wasn't just about achievement. It was a deep-seated desire for more. A yearning for purpose, for every moment to resonate with meaning.

There's a vivid memory of days spent in my basement bedroom, shared with my brother Jimmy. With baseball commentary ringing in the background, I'd hurl tennis balls against the cement walls, each thud a testament to my passion. Each angle, a simulated position in the game. Later, as I evolved into a BMX freestyle rider, my ambitions soared, quite literally. In the sweltering heat of Northbridge Mass, I pushed my boundaries, levitating higher off ramps, challenging myself to match and then surpass global benchmarks. From 6 feet to an exhilarating 11 feet, my journey was marked by grit and perseverance.

This tenacity didn't just remain confined to sports; it permeated my business endeavors. The path to success, as most would attest, is strewn with failures. Yet, the key lies not in the falls, but in the countless times we rise. Every venture, every dream, has its dark alleys where the end seems elusive. Yet, on most days, I could glimpse the proverbial light at the end of the tunnel.

The true essence of accomplishment isn't just about achieving a goal. It's about those subconscious triggers that jolt us into action, the reminders of our purpose and path. Embarking on this journey, one must realize it's often a solitary quest. While some companions might join for a while, buoying spirits and catalyzing growth, paths diverge. And the transient nature of such partnerships can sting, especially when shared moments have been profoundly enriching. Yet, with every parting, a new chapter beckons, laden with fresh experiences and revelations.

In essence, every individual's "cause of accomplishment" is unique, shaped by their experiences and aspirations. Through this chapter, while I've shared slices of my own journey, the hope is for readers to discern their own triggers, their own paths, and craft their distinctive narratives of achievement.

Figure:1.10:

The Cause of Accomplishment

THE DIRT IS IN THE DETAILS

The adage "The devil is in the details" isn't just a mere saying—it's a potent truth that's especially relevant in our journey towards "The cause of accomplishment." Drawing parallels to our earlier discussions, let's delve into why being meticulous matters, especially when it comes to optimizing your online presence and your real-life endeavors.

In the digital realm, the analogy of 'ranking' doesn't just mean showing up on search engines; it translates to how well you articulate your business's essence. Think of the internet as a vast marketplace where everyone is vying for attention. But how do you ensure that you stand out? It's not merely about being present; it's about being remarkable, memorable, and most importantly, relevant.

Every business, every brand, every individual has a unique selling proposition (USP). Pinpointing and emphasizing this USP requires a deep dive into the details of what you offer. By focusing keenly on the nuances of your products or services, you ensure that they aren't just noticed—they're appreciated and sought after.

Let's take keywords, for instance. In the digital marketing world, keywords are more than just search terms. They are gateways to human desires, needs, and aspirations. When a potential customer types in a keyword, they aren't just looking for a product; they're looking for a solution, an experience, or even a transformation. By giving meticulous attention to the details of these keywords, you are, in essence, tapping into the very psyche of your potential customer base. You're acknowledging their needs and signaling that you have exactly what they're looking for.

This principle applies beyond the digital sphere and seeps into the physical realm of businesses. The meticulousness with which you craft your products, design your storefront, or even train your staff, all these details culminate in creating an unparalleled experience for your customers. It's the difference between a diner remembering a meal and a diner raving about the culinary journey they just embarked on.

Tying it back to "The cause of accomplishment," this unwavering focus on details is what propels individuals and businesses forward. It's about recognizing the granular components that make up the bigger picture and refining them to perfection.

However, it's essential to strike a balance. While it's crucial to get into the weeds and understand every tiny aspect, it's equally vital not to lose sight of the broader vision. The details should always serve the bigger picture, not overshadow it.

Whether you're building a brand, writing a book, or crafting a software, it's the intricate details that can set you apart. When woven together, these details narrate a compelling story—a story of passion, dedication, and an unwavering commitment to excellence. So, as you tread on your path towards accomplishment, remember to dig deep into the details, for within them lies the magic that can set you apart.

The Cause of Accomplishment

THE 15%...

In the vast sea of digital knowledge and the endless tides of online courses, there is an island that only a few manage to reach. It's the island of completion, the place where the 15% dwell—those rare individuals who don't just start a course but see it through to the very end. The path to this island is not hidden; it's simply that few choose to travel it to completion.

My neighbor Noah, the man who seems to be a marketing savant and a spring of ceaseless energy, handed me the compass to this island. Our conversations are like a storm of insights, each word another gust pushing me closer to understanding the intricacies of SEO. Noah's approach to business direction is nothing short of supernatural, and getting a slice of his time feels like uncovering treasure. Each interaction leaves me richer in knowledge.

The day Noah gave voice to the stark statistic that only 15% of people finish the courses they buy, it hit me like a lightning bolt. The concept was familiar, but the reality of it had never truly sunk in. It wasn't just a figure; it represented a mindset, a division between the many who aspire and the few who achieve.

You see, everything that went into the fabric of my software, RankingMastery, is a patchwork of the strategies and insights Noah shared with me. His fingerprints are on its blueprints, making his surprise at the completion rates all the more poignant. Noah completes what he starts, and his success is a testament to that relentless pursuit.

Now, as you turn these pages, consider yourself part of an ongoing case study. Will you step across the threshold and commit to being part of that 15%? As you journey through this book, and perhaps through the accompanying course, you are at a crossroads.

I draw inspiration from my love for golf—a sport where to score in the 70s means entering the top 1% of players worldwide. That exclusivity, that elite echelon, is what drives me to improve my swing, to study the course, to practice tirelessly. It's not just about playing; it's about excelling among the best.

Ask yourself: Do you simply want to play the game, or do you strive to score among the best? Do you want to be a part of the majority who start with enthusiasm but fade into the background, or do you want to be among the persistent few who press forward to mastery?

I leave you with this challenge not just as a motivator, but as a reflection of reality. Finishing this book, applying its principles, and completing the RankingMastery course could redefine the trajectory of your business and personal growth. I urge you to chase that top 1%, to be relentless in your pursuit, and to recognize that in the world of SEO and online marketing, as in golf, the sweetest victories are those hard-earned and rare.

So, as I close this chapter and head out to the golf course, I wonder: Will you be joining me in the ranks of the 15%? Will your name be etched among the doers, the finishers, the masters? The next chapter awaits, and so does your decision.

AI: UN REAL, REMARKABLE, BEYOND BELIEF

WHAT IS AI TO YOU

As you delve into the world of SEO, aiming to become a "RankingMaster," you'll find that artificial intelligence, like ChatGPT, is an invaluable resource in your toolkit. The journey toward mastering the art of ranking on search engines is multifaceted, involving an understanding of complex algorithms, the creation of captivating content, and the implementation of effective strategies. This is where leveraging AI can give you a significant edge.

AI can serve as an analytical tool and a creative partner. It can simplify the complex, often overwhelming world of SEO into digestible, actionable steps. For example, when you're faced with the daunting task of keyword research, AI can streamline the process, offering up a curated list of keywords that can propel your content to the top of search results. When it comes to crafting compelling articles, blog posts, or web pages, AI can assist in generating initial drafts, suggesting improvements, and ensuring that your content is optimized for both search engines and human engagement.

But AI's capabilities don't stop at content creation. It's also equipped to perform content analysis, providing feedback that can elevate the quality of your existing material. This includes optimizing meta tags, enhancing your backlink profile, and refining the overall structure of your site to be more search engine friendly.

Link building, a critical aspect of SEO, can also benefit from AI's insights. AI can help identify potential link-building opportunities, drawing from a vast database of online resources and strategies that have proven effective across various industries. It can simulate the process of network expansion and the value of forging digital connections that bolster your site's credibility.

Moreover, AI can be utilized to conduct comprehensive competitor analysis. It can pinpoint what your competitors are doing right, where there are gaps in their strategies, and how you can uniquely position yourself to capitalize on these insights.

Incorporating AI into your SEO strategy is not about replacing the human touch; rather, it's about enhancing your capabilities and allowing you to focus on the creative and human aspects of your business. AI is a powerful ally in the ever-evolving landscape of online marketing, and by harnessing its potential, you can pave your way to becoming a true "RankingMaster."

By embracing AI in your SEO endeavors, you can demystify the complexities of search engine algorithms, elevate your content, and execute strategies that lead to lasting success in the digital domain.

AI: Un real, Remarkable, Beyond Belief

BUSINESS PROFILER

As a pioneering guide for utilizing AI in your SEO and marketing efforts, I've crafted a series of scripts that you can use to jumpstart your journey with AI assistance. These scripts are designed to streamline the process of creating a comprehensive SEO profile for your business, "Readers Company," and can be adapted to fit any client's needs. Let's explore these scripts and how you can leverage them:

Industry Analysis Script: "Please conduct a niche market analysis for 'Readers Company' that includes a business overview, target market identification, potential service offerings, market needs assessment, growth potential areas, unique selling proposition (USP), and a concluding summary."

Ideal Customer Profile Script: "Generate a detailed report on the ideal customer profile for 'Readers Company', focusing on demographics, business-to-business client characteristics, behavioral traits, purchasing motivations, and a conclusion summarizing these findings."

Benefits and Features Script: "Create a comprehensive report outlining the core benefits and features of 'Readers Company', specifically tailored to their industry, and provide a conclusion that encapsulates the primary advantages."

Marketing Strategy Script: "Develop a marketing strategy for 'Readers Company' that outlines the target audience, current market positioning versus competitors, five innovative branding suggestions, five traditional marketing ideas, an actionable plan, and a concluding overview."

SEO Keyword Strategy Script: "Propose a set of 20 SEO-driven keyword phrases specifically curated to enhance targeted content creation for 'Readers Company', aimed at driving traffic and increasing engagement."

Domain Name Proposals Script: "Suggest 20 SEO-optimized domain names for 'Readers Company' that incorporate the most popular keywords within their niche market."

Client Objections Inventory Script: "List potential reservations or objections that clients of 'Readers Company' might have, alongside strategic responses to each."

Website Content Direction Script: "Outline a content strategy for 'Readers Company' that addresses the value proposition, details the service offerings, and recommends calls to action that effectively capture leads, such as opt-ins, webinars, or free consultations."

Website Framework Script: "Recommend an intuitive structure for 'Readers Company's' website that prioritizes user experience and lead conversion optimization."

Key Client Questions Script: "Identify the top 10 questions clients are likely to ask about 'Readers Company's' services and offerings."

Call to Action Script: "Craft five unique and compelling calls to action that encourage potential clients to engage with 'Readers Company'."

Opt-In Landing Page Thank You Email Script: "Compose a thoughtful 'Thank You' email for 'Readers Company' that will be sent to new subscribers, reaffirming their decision to engage and providing further steps for interaction."

Promotional Video Outline Script: "Create a promotional video outline for 'Readers Company' that they can execute using their mobile phone, incorporating 'The Hero's Journey' narrative structure, and tailored for a low-budget production."

Each script is a starting point—a template that you can use to harness the power of AI for your SEO and marketing efforts. By employing these scripts, you ensure that 'Readers Company' not only forges ahead in the SEO realm but also captivates and converts its audience through strategic content and structured marketing initiatives.

ARE YOU AN EXPERT OR SIDE GIG

THE POWER OF BEING THE GOTO EXPERT

In the vast ecosystem of business, there's an apex position that many aim for but few truly grasp: being the undisputed "go-to" expert in one's field. The journey to this pinnacle isn't just about prestige or recognition; it translates into tangible benefits that can catapult your business and personal brand to uncharted heights.

Imagine this: You walk into a room filled with professionals from your industry. While many are competent and knowledgeable, only a few radiate that aura of unassailable expertise. These are the people others gravitate toward, seeking insights, guidance, and partnership. Now, what if I told you that you could be that magnet in the room?

First, let's debunk a myth: Expertise isn't reserved for those with a trail of degrees or decades in the industry. Many times, expertise comes from on-the-ground experience, the intuitive understanding of nuances, the hard-earned lessons from challenges faced and overcome.

Consider this: You've been honing your craft for years, encountering unique problems and crafting solutions. Each of those moments has bestowed upon you a wealth of knowledge. Those street secrets, the shortcuts you've discovered, the loopholes you've exploited, or even the warnings you can share—they are goldmines. They could prevent a startup from making a costly error or guide a veteran business through a tricky pivot. Recognizing and valuing this knowledge is the first step toward establishing yourself as the go-to expert.

So, what does being the "go-to" expert entail?

1. Commanding Premium Pricing: Expertise has a price tag. When clients realize they're getting advice or services backed by unparalleled experience and insight, they're willing to pay a premium. It's similar to choosing a specialist surgeon over a general practitioner for a complex procedure. The assurance of quality and outcomes justifies the cost.

2. Opening Doors to Speaking Engagements: As the recognized authority in your field, you're not just another voice; you're THE voice. Organizations, seminars, and conferences will seek you out, offering platforms to share your insights, thereby amplifying your reach and influence.

3. Building Trust and Credibility: Being the expert means clients come to you with trust already built in. Your reputation precedes you. This trust shortens sales cycles, enhances client relationships, and bolsters your brand's value.

Now, the compelling question is, how do you start on this journey to becoming the go-to expert? Begin with self-awareness. Understand and catalogue your unique experiences and insights. Document your journey, your learnings, your successes, and even your failures. Share them, whether it's through blogs, videos, podcasts, or seminars. Engage with your industry, be it through webinars, panel discussions, or collaborative projects.

In essence, the road to being the "go-to" expert isn't about grand gestures but consistent, small steps. Each piece of content shared, each interaction, and each collaboration builds upon the last, forging your path to expertise. The world needs your unique insights and experience. It's time to step into your power and claim your position as the authority in your field.

WEAVING EXPERTISE INTO YOUR MARKETING - THE REAL-WORLD RANK

In the digital era, there's an immense focus on 'ranking'—ascending the ladder of search results to grab that coveted top spot. But what often gets overlooked is the parallel ladder, one that's climbed in the real world through expertise and authority. This chapter ties these two concepts together, reinforcing how the prowess of your real-world standing can significantly amplify your digital rank.

Let's start by considering a simple truth: People prefer to do business with those they recognize as authorities. If two services appear in a search, and one is offered by a known expert, that service is almost guaranteed to attract more attention, even if it ranks slightly lower in search results. This is where "RankingMastery" steps in, bridging the gap between your real-world expertise and your digital visibility.

Ranking on the internet is crucial, but it's only part of the equation. Your digital rank can get a potential client to your website, but it's your real-world expertise that will convert them. When a visitor sees articles, videos, or testimonials that underscore your depth of knowledge and experience, they're more likely to trust, engage, and eventually become a loyal client.

Think of it this way: Your digital rank gets you to the dance, but your expertise is what makes people want to dance with you.

The beauty of "RankingMastery" is its ability to seamlessly blend these worlds. By harnessing the platform, you're not just optimizing for search engines but also for the human psyche, intuitively understanding what your potential clients seek.

But here's the catch: Just as in the world of SEO where keyword-stuffed content without value is penalized, in the real world, claims of expertise without substance will be equally disregarded. This is where the genuine weaving of your expertise into your marketing becomes paramount. Every piece of content should echo your authority, knowledge, and the unique value you bring to the table.

In essence, the symbiotic relationship between your real-world expertise and your digital rank cannot be emphasized enough. By marrying the two, not only do you elevate your digital visibility but also solidify your standing in the real-world marketplace. With "RankingMastery" as your ally, you have a powerful tool that underscores this synergy, propelling you to unparalleled heights in both realms.

So, as we delve deeper into this chapter, remember: Your rank in the real world, built on the bedrock of genuine expertise, is as critical, if not more so, than your digital rank. In the intricate dance of business success, mastering both these rhythms is the key to an impeccable performance.

Are you an Expert or Side Gig

THE EXPERT'S PLAYBOOK: ACTIONS THAT SOLIDIFY AUTHORITY

What comes to mind when you think of the term 'expert'? Perhaps it's an author signing their latest book, a consultant giving a keynote speech, or a specialist being interviewed on national television. These aren't mere perceptions; they are very much the reality, actions that experts commonly engage in to reinforce their authority and widen their impact. As we venture into the following chapters, we'll dissect each of these endeavors in detail, providing a vivid insight into what real-world experts do to stand out.

1. Writing Books: There's a reason the phrase "wrote the book on it" signifies expertise. Authoring a book on your area of specialization not only reaffirms your authority but also allows you to reach a wider audience. A well-written book serves as both a business card and a resume,

providing tangible proof of your in-depth knowledge and experience.

2. Creating Courses: With the rise of online learning platforms, there's never been a better time for experts to share their knowledge through structured courses. By designing and promoting a course, you're not just augmenting your revenue streams but also underlining your role as an industry leader.

3. Making News Appearances: The media is always on the lookout for authoritative voices, especially when a story aligns with a specific niche. Experts who foster relationships with journalists and media establishments find themselves at the helm when news in their domain emerges, offering invaluable insights and benefiting from vast exposure.

4. Starting a Podcast: Podcasting has seen a meteoric rise in popularity. It presents experts with a platform to delve deep into subjects, interview fellow thought leaders, and engage with a devoted audience. With every episode, you cement your reputation further and grow your listener base.

5. Creating Events: Be it a workshop, seminar, or a larger conference, events are avenues for experts to connect with their audience, showcase their prowess, and establish stronger networks. Moreover, a successfully orchestrated

event can significantly uplift your brand's stature in your industry.

Each of these actions is a pivotal step in an expert's journey, serving as gateways to broader audiences, platforms to disseminate knowledge, and mediums to amplify your brand's influence.

In the upcoming chapters, we'll delve deep into the nuances of each of these avenues, equipping you with a blueprint to incorporate them into your ascent, evolving from a practitioner to an unrivaled expert in your field.

Are you an Expert or Side Gig

TAKING THE LEAP: EMBRACING THE EXPERT WITHIN YOU

The prospect of stepping into the spotlight as an expert can be daunting. But remember, expertise isn't just about how much you know—it's about how you share that knowledge with others. By authoring a book, creating courses, making news appearances, hosting a podcast, or organizing events, you're not only showcasing your expertise but also adding value to your community, industry, and beyond.

Perhaps you're wondering: "Do I really have what it takes?" Let me assure you; the very fact that you're reading this indicates an innate drive and potential. Your years of experience, the challenges you've overcome, the knowledge you've gained, and the unique perspective you offer—these are all invaluable.

1. Start Small, Dream Big: You don't need to pen a 500-page book as your first step. Begin with a series of articles or blog

posts on topics you're passionate about. Over time, these can be the foundation of a more extensive publication.

2. Share Your Journey: The story of your career, the ups and downs, the lessons learned along the way, can be the core of a course or workshop. Remember, people don't just buy expertise; they buy experiences and relatability.

3. Engage With Your Audience: You'd be surprised at how much people want to hear from industry insiders. Start a monthly webinar, Q&A sessions, or even informal coffee chats. These can eventually evolve into podcasts or more extensive speaking engagements.

4. Collaborate: Network with fellow professionals. Co-host a podcast, write a joint article, or organize an event together. Collaboration not only divides the work but multiplies the results.

5. Keep Learning: The world is constantly evolving. By staying updated, attending workshops, or taking courses yourself, you're ensuring that your expertise remains relevant and in demand.

In the words of the renowned author Neale Donald Walsch, "Life begins at the end of your comfort zone." Don't wait for a sign or the 'perfect' moment. Your expertise is your currency, and the world needs it. Dive into the deep end. Start with one, or embrace them all. The journey from where you are to becoming a recognized expert in your field is filled with opportunities, learning, and growth. Embrace it, for the rewards—both tangible and intangible—are beyond measure.

COLORS AND BRANDING AND MORE

THE WEBSITE'S WARDROBE – THE IMPACT OF COLOR PALETTES

Imagine walking into a room where every piece of furniture, every wall color, every fabric, somehow, magically, harmoniously blends together. There's an unseen pull, a magnetism that doesn't shout but rather whispers its elegance. Your website, at its best, should evoke a similar reaction. It's more than just a digital platform; it's a representation of your brand's personality and vision. Just as you'd dress to impress for an important meeting, your website must be dressed to impress every visitor. This is where the art and science of color palettes come into play.

1. The Emotional Quotient of Colors

Colors aren't just visual elements; they are emotional triggers. Think about it. Does the color blue remind you of a calm ocean or sky, making you feel at peace? Does red ignite passion, energy, and urgency? Every color has a psychological effect. For businesses, understanding these subtleties is crucial. If your brand aims to convey trust and calmness, shades of blue might dominate your palette. On the flip side, a fast-food joint might employ vibrant reds and yellows to indicate speed, energy, and zest.

2. The Art of Contrast and Readability

Contrasting colors aren't just for aesthetic appeal; they enhance the functionality of your site. The right contrast ensures that your text is readable against its background. For instance, a white font on a pastel background might look ethereal but can strain your reader's eyes. A dark blue font, however, would stand out and be easily readable.

3. The Flow and Unity of Design

Just as in fashion, where too many clashing prints can be overwhelming, an overabundance of colors can create visual chaos on a site. A well-thought-out color palette establishes flow and unity. It guides the visitor's eye, highlighting essential points, and ensuring a smooth journey through the content.

4. Consistency and Branding

The colors you choose become synonymous with your brand's identity. Think of the iconic Tiffany blue or the bold red of Coca-Cola. Over time, these colors become instantly recognizable symbols of the brand. A consistent color palette across your website reinforces brand identity and ensures that visitors identify the colors with your business.

5. Tips for Curating Your Palette

If you're starting from scratch, take inspiration from your business values, your target audience, and current design trends. Use tools like Adobe Color or Coolors to experiment with different combinations. Consider the 60-30-10 rule: 60% primary color, 30% secondary color, and 10% accent color. And always keep accessibility in mind – ensure that your website is visually accessible to everyone, including those with color vision deficiencies.

While compelling content is the backbone of any website, the color palette is its skin, its face, its attire. It's what makes the first impression, holds attention, and remains memorable long after the visit. So, just as you'd take time choosing the perfect outfit for a grand occasion, invest time and thought into curating the perfect color palette for your website. Let your site not just speak but shine.

Colors and Branding and More

THE 'THREE SECOND RULE' - MASTERING VISUAL IMPACT

In a world where attention is the new currency, the 'Three Second Rule' isn't just a principle; it's the cornerstone of effective web design. It's the understanding that within three seconds, your website must make an impact, or risk losing a potential customer to the abyss of the internet. Let's explore how to apply this rule to create a visually impactful website that not only captures attention but drives action.

Part 1: The Quick Glance Test

To master the 'Three Second Rule', begin with the 'Quick Glance Test'. Open the webpage you want to optimize and look at it for precisely three seconds, then quickly shut your eyes. In that instant, what sticks? The elements you recall are your visual anchors—these could be your headline, a striking image, or your call to action. They're what your visitors will notice first and remember most.

Part 2: Ensuring Clarity of Message

When you reopen your eyes for another three seconds, ask yourself: Is the message clear? Do the most memorable elements convey the problem you're solving or the value you're offering? If your unique value proposition isn't part of what stands out, it's time to revisit your design hierarchy. The goal of your visual layout should be to make the path to understanding as short and as clear as possible.

Part 3: Highlighting the Call to Action

The 'Three Second Rule' is particularly crucial for your call to action (CTA). After the brief viewing, does the CTA make an impression? If it doesn't, it's lost in the visual noise. Consider its size, color, and placement. The CTA needs to be a natural next step for your visitors, standing out without overwhelming the surrounding content.

Part 4: Designing for Conversion

Designing with the 'Three Second Rule' in mind is about creating pages that lead to conversion. Each element must be carefully considered—not just for aesthetic appeal, but for its role in the visitor's journey. Every image, every block of text, every button is a signpost directing your users where you want them to go.

Part 5: Iterative Improvement

Finally, remember that the 'Three Second Rule' is not a one-time check. It's an iterative process. As you add content, as trends change, as your business evolves, keep applying this rule. By doing so, you ensure that your site remains focused, fresh, and above all, effective at converting visitors into customers.

In conclusion, the 'Three Second Rule' is an exercise in simplicity and focus. It's about stripping away the superfluous and honing in on what matters most. Whether you're a seasoned designer or a business owner crafting your own site, this rule helps ensure that every visitor's fleeting attention is captured and directed towards the action that benefits your business the most.

Colors and Branding and More

MARGIN AND PADDING

While the 'Three Second Rule' revolves around immediate visual impact, spacing plays a significant role in ensuring that impact is as powerful as it can be. Just as silence can emphasize sound in music, white space (or negative space) can emphasize content in web design. This space isn't always "white," of course—it's just free from text, images, or embellishments.

Part 1: The Power of Spacing

A cluttered webpage can be overwhelming. It's similar to trying to read a book where the words are crammed edge to edge, without margins or breaks between paragraphs. The content might be compelling, but the presentation is off-putting. Proper spacing gives each design element its own "room to breathe," making it more noticeable, digestible, and memorable.

Part 2: Margin vs. Padding - The Subtle Art

Understanding the difference between margin and padding is crucial:

- Margin: Think of margin as the 'personal space' of a design element. It pushes other elements away on the outside. By adjusting the margin, you can ensure elements are distinctly separate from one another, giving each its own space on the stage.

- Padding: Padding serves as an 'internal cushion' for a design element. If your element is a box with a background color, padding determines the space between the content inside the box (like text or an image) and the edges of that box. Proper padding ensures content inside an element is readable and visually appealing, and doesn't feel cramped.

Part 3: Spacing for Readability and Aesthetics

Proper spacing isn't just about aesthetics; it's about readability and functionality. When text and elements have sufficient space, users can skim and scan more efficiently. Spacing ensures that clickable elements, like buttons or links, are easily distinguishable and tappable, especially on mobile devices.

Part 4: Consistency is Key

Ensure consistent spacing throughout your webpage. If you've decided on a 20-pixel margin between elements in one section, try to apply that consistently across similar sections. This creates a rhythm and balance, making your website appear professional and well-thought-out.

The beauty of spacing lies in its subtlety. While it might seem like a minor detail, it has a profound effect on the overall user experience. By mastering the art of spacing, combined with the 'Three Second Rule', you're ensuring your content is not just seen but also enjoyed and remembered.

THE RIGHT IMAGES ARE ASSETS

THE ART OF IMAGERY: CRAFTING A VISUAL STORY FOR YOUR BRAND

We live in a visually-driven world. From the feeds of our social media platforms to the billboards we pass on the highway, imagery plays a monumental role in influencing our decisions and shaping our perceptions. This chapter delves into the powerful influence of images, especially in the digital realm, and the undeniable impact they have on branding, trust-building, and storytelling.

Imagine for a moment walking into an art gallery. Each painting tells a story, evoking emotions and sparking thoughts without saying a word. This silent communication is precisely what your brand needs — a visual narrative that speaks volumes.

1. First Impressions Matter: We've all heard the saying, "Don't judge a book by its cover." Yet, more often than not, we do. A pixelated, irrelevant, or outdated image can instantly erode the

credibility of your website or marketing campaign. On the flip side, a sharp, purposeful, and captivating image can draw a viewer in, compelling them to engage with your content.

2. Colors, Moods, and Emotions: Every hue elicits an emotion. The vibrancy of a red 'Sale' tag, the calm of a blue ocean background, or the trust instilled by a green certification seal – colors are a language unto themselves. Professional images ensure that the color palette aligns with your brand's message and ethos.

3. Simplifying Design and Message: A great image reduces the need for excessive design elements. It becomes the centerpiece, drawing attention and conveying the primary message. When your visuals are strong, you can let them do the talking, often simplifying and decluttering your website's overall design.

4. Boosting Trust and Credibility: We trust what looks good. High-quality, professional photos lend credibility to your brand, making it appear more established and trustworthy. Whether you're showcasing a product, offering a service, or sharing a testimonial, clear and appealing visuals can tip the scale in your favor.

5. The Universality of Visuals: While language barriers can often be a hurdle, images are universal. They transcend linguistic confines, reaching out and resonating with a global audience.

In conclusion, as you journey through building or refining your brand's digital presence, remember the art and science behind images. Your visuals aren't just placeholders – they're powerful storytellers, brand ambassadors, and trust builders. Investing in professional images isn't just an aesthetic choice; it's a strategic move, a commitment to quality, and a nod to the discerning nature of today's consumer. As the adage goes, "A picture is worth a thousand words." Ensure those words resonate, inspire, and convert by prioritizing top-notch imagery.

The Right Images are Assets

HARNESSING THE PHOTOGRAPHIC MIGHT OF MODERN CELL PHONES

In today's digitized era, one of the most transformative inventions has been the cell phone. Beyond calling and texting, these devices have evolved into powerful multimedia tools, with their camera functionalities being a standout feature. It's fascinating to think that the little device in your pocket could rival the quality of professional cameras from just a few years ago. Let's explore how to make the most of your smartphone's camera capabilities, especially when professional photography might be beyond reach.

1. Quality Beyond Belief: Modern smartphones, be it the latest iPhone or a top-tier Android device, boast camera specifications that are nothing short of incredible. With many featuring upwards of 18 megapixels, and some even touching the 100-megapixel mark, the clarity and detail they can capture are genuinely astounding. This isn't just about numbers; it's about the stunning images those numbers translate into.

2. Cinematic Video on a Budget: If you've ever marveled at the sweeping cinematic shots in movies and thought, "I wish I could do that," your phone might just be your answer. Features like slow motion, time-lapse, stabilization, and 4K recording can help you produce video content that's high on quality without being heavy on your wallet.

3. Professional Features: HDR, Portrait Mode, Night Mode, and Pro-level manual settings — modern smartphones come equipped with features that were once exclusive to high-end cameras. These tools empower users to capture shots with dynamic ranges, blurred backgrounds, clear low-light pictures, and much more, enabling a touch of professionalism in every click.

4. The World of Apps: The App Store and Google Play Store are treasure troves for photography enthusiasts. From advanced editing tools like Adobe Lightroom and VSCO to specialized camera apps that offer granular control over settings, the possibilities are endless.

5. Instant Sharing and Cloud Storage: One advantage cell phones have over traditional cameras is the ecosystem they belong to. Clicked a fantastic shot? Share it instantly on social media, get feedback, make edits, or store it securely on the cloud. The entire process is streamlined and efficient.

6. Learning Curve: While having a capable device is half the battle, knowing how to use it to its full potential is equally crucial. Fortunately, there's a plethora of online tutorials, courses,

and forums dedicated to smartphone photography, ensuring you're never left fumbling in the dark.

In conclusion, while there's undeniable allure in professional cameras and their myriad lenses, it's heartening to know that for many businesses and individuals, a smartphone can serve as a potent photography tool. The key lies in understanding its capabilities and learning to harness them effectively. Remember, in the realm of content creation, especially for businesses, authenticity often trumps perfection. Your smartphone, with its ever-ready camera, allows you to capture and share moments as they unfold, making your brand story feel real, immediate, and relatable.

MAKING CONNECTIONS

SOMETHING YOU ARE FAMILIAR WITH

In the digital expanse, your reach, influence, and authority are often defined not just by the content you create but also by the company you keep. Much like the intricate dance of social standing in the real world, where connections can open doors and create opportunities, the virtual world operates on the currency of credibility and association. This is the essence of link building—a fundamental aspect of SEO that goes beyond mere strategy; it's the digital equivalent of networking and reputation building.

Forging Digital Relationships Link building is a delicate art. It's similar to extending a handshake in the virtual world. Just as you would at a networking event, where you engage with peers, share insights, and exchange business cards, online link building involves reaching out to fellow webmasters, bloggers, and influencers to create a mutually beneficial connection. The aim is to weave a tapestry of links that not only draws users to your site but also signals to search engines the value and relevance of your content.

Establishing Credibility In the physical world, our reputations are often shaped by who endorses us, who we associate with, and who we know. On the internet, search engines like Google take note of similar endorsements. When a reputable site links to your content, it's as if they're telling the search engines, "This content is trustworthy; this source is credible." It's a vouch for quality that can elevate your site's standing in the intricate hierarchy of search results.

The Hierarchy of Digital Respect Just as society might confer more respect on certain titles and positions, the digital world confers authority on certain types of links. A link from a prestigious university's website (.edu), a government portal (.gov), or an established non-profit (.org) carries a weight similar to an endorsement from a trusted public figure or institution. These links are hard-earned badges of honor, and they can significantly impact your site's SEO and perceived trustworthiness.

To command respect and authority online, it's not enough to just exist in isolation. Your site must be part of a broader conversation, a living, breathing ecosystem where each link serves as a pathway to greater understanding and context. The quality of your connections—of your links—echoes the quality of your content and by extension, your brand.

Navigating this web of digital connections requires tact, strategy, and a genuine desire to contribute value. It's not just about seeking links for the sake of numbers; it's about building genuine relationships that enrich the web and provide users with the best possible experience. As in life, so in the digital realm: the strength and quality of your relationships define your journey and success.

As you search into the world of link building, consider each potential link as you would a potential ally or partner. Seek out those who share your values, who can amplify your voice, and who can help you build a platform of credibility and authority. With each connection forged, you're not just building links; you're building your legacy in the digital world.

Making Connections

MY LIFE TRANSLATED INTO LINKS

n the spirited world of BMX Freestyle, where every trick and every jump builds your reputation, my journey as a professional rider taught me the value of connections—both on the ground and in the air. Each competition, each display of skill was an opportunity to establish links with sponsors, fellow athletes, and fans. These connections, these human 'links,' propelled my career, opening doors to new opportunities and higher platforms.

Similarly, as a podcaster, the conversations I've had with guests, the networks I've tapped into, have all been about establishing connections. Each episode is a link in a chain that extends my reach, enhances my influence, and builds my credibility. My guests, often individuals of significant standing in their respective fields, lend their voices to my show, which, in turn, becomes an endorsement of my platform.

Now, let's translate this to the online realm. In the digital landscape, every backlink from a reputable source is like having an influential figure endorse you in the BMX world or a renowned guest appear on your podcast. It's a signal to both search engines and potential listeners or customers that you're a figure of authority and trustworthiness.

For instance, imagine a scenario where a major BMX brand links to your personal website following an interview or a high-profile event. This link is a testament to your standing in the BMX community. It tells your audience and search engines alike that you're a credible figure, one that a leading brand recognizes and associates with. The credibility that comes with it is invaluable—it's not something you can create with just good content or savvy search engine optimization alone.

In the world of podcasting, each time a guest shares their interview with their audience, it creates a new pathway back to my platform. These digital endorsements spread my reach further than I could achieve alone. They're affirmations of the value I provide, mirroring the nods of approval from the crowd when landing a new trick on the BMX track.

The lesson here is clear: in life, as in the digital world, the connections you forge define your path and propel you forward. My life as a BMX Freestyler and a podcaster has been a testament to that. The 'links' I've built have not only expanded my personal horizons but have also amplified my digital presence. They are the bridges between my content and my audience, and they reinforce my status as an influencer in both arenas.

Just as every successful stunt in BMX was a result of practice, precision, and a bit of daring, every successful link is a combination of quality content, strategic outreach, and the courage to put your work out there. As you navigate the world of SEO and online marketing, think of link building as you would building a network in any professional venture—it's about creating genuine connections that hold the weight of credibility and authority.

Making Connections

TRANSLATE YOUR LIFE INTO LINKS

As you sit back and survey the expanse of your digital world, it's time for a moment of introspection. Look closely at the life and business you've built—every piece of content you've created, every interaction you've had, every profile you've established. These aren't just isolated moments or stand-alone assets; they're potential links, conduits that can lead back to your digital domain, your website.

Your journey through life and business is rich with link-building opportunities. The videos you've uploaded to YouTube, the photos and stories on Instagram, the insightful threads on Twitter, and the deep-diving episodes of your podcast—all these are breadcrumbs on your treasure map. Each one holds the potential to guide visitors back to your site, enhancing its visibility and credibility.

Consider the 'Treasure Map Mode' as your approach to uncovering these opportunities. Every social media post can be more than a message; it can be a signpost pointing to your website. Each video can be more than a story; it can be a path to your services or products. Your podcasts aren't just conversations;

they are invitations for listeners to explore further, to delve deeper into the world you've created.

Take inventory of what you have, where you've been, and who you know. In every corner of your digital presence lies hidden treasure, waiting to be claimed. Just as a treasure map teases the promise of undiscovered riches, your inventory teases the promise of untapped potential—links waiting to be forged, relationships waiting to be leveraged, and credibility waiting to be built.

It's about being proactive, about being in 'Treasure Map Mode' all the time. It's about recognizing that the webinar you guested on, the industry forum where you contributed valuable insights, the online community where you're an active member—all these can translate into backlinks that reinforce the ranking of your website.

This isn't just a game of numbers; it's a strategic quest for quality connections that align with your brand's ethos and audience's needs. It's about creating a network so interwoven with your professional narrative that your website becomes the natural nexus of your online activities.

So, embark on this quest. Comb through your digital interactions, sift through your content, and start the process of linking back to your website. With every link you establish, you're not just improving your SEO; you're crafting a story, a narrative that resonates with authenticity and authority. Let each link be a step closer to the treasure you seek—greater visibility, higher ranking, and a business that thrives in the digital world.

Making Connections

PHONE CONTACTS

In the rich tapestry of our social and professional lives, our phone's address book is a microcosm of our world—a hive of connections, each contact an intersection of stories, opportunities, and shared histories. It's fascinating to ponder how your own name, embedded within the address books of others, forms a node in a vast network, linking you to an intricate web of interconnections that span far beyond your immediate circle.

This web of contacts—of friends, colleagues, mentors, and acquaintances—reflects a matrix of relationships, each with the potential to influence and shape your journey. Just as a single thread can alter the pattern of a weave, a single contact can open up new avenues, introduce new ideas, and shift your social standing. Your name, nestled amongst hundreds of others, carries your reputation, your personal brand, and your potential to influence.

In this digital age, the concept of 'networking' extends well beyond the confines of our physical interactions. Each entry in your address book represents not just a person but a potential link in your professional web—a link that could lead to a new career opportunity, a collaborative project, or a pivotal introduction. And just like the physical address book, your digital presence—be it through your social media profiles, email contacts, or professional platforms like LinkedIn—is a testament to the breadth and depth of your network.

These networks, both digital and physical, underscore the importance of fostering meaningful connections. They remind us that our social standing and professional success are often not just the result of individual effort but the product of collaborative synergy. Each contact in your address book, each link in your network, holds the latent power to impact your real-life standing—each is a chance for interaction, for engagement, and ultimately, for growth.

So as you consider the value of each name, each number, and each email address you've collected over the years, think about how these points of contact form your unique web of opportunities. Reflect on how you can nurture these connections, how you can enrich this network, and how you can expand this web to support your aspirations and ambitions. After all, in the interconnected world of today, your network is more than just a list of names—it's a living, evolving entity that holds the key to your social and professional elevation.

ALIGN YOURSELF WITH THE RIGHT PEOPLE

HOW I ALIGNED MYSELF WITH INFLUENTIAL FIGURES

Having a signature avatar creates an immediate visual association, setting the stage for brand recognition. But beyond this visual cue, there's tremendous power in the relationships you cultivate, especially with influential figures in your niche. Such associations don't just validate your brand, but they also open new avenues of opportunity. Here's a roadmap, illustrated with personal anecdotes, on how you can initiate and foster these priceless connections.

1. Starting Small:
Building a relationship with influential figures often starts with small, seemingly insignificant gestures. Something as simple as taking a photo with them can be the genesis of a deeper connection. This photograph not only serves as a memorable token but can be a conversation starter in future engagements.

2. Being Genuinely Curious:

People, irrespective of their stature, appreciate genuine interest. Asking personal or insightful questions can pave the way for a deeper connection. It shows that you see beyond their public persona, valuing the individual behind the fame.

3. My Journey at Funnel Hacking Live:

I found myself amidst a sea of potential connections at Funnel Hacking Live, a grand event orchestrated by Clickfunnels. Rather than being a passive attendee, I made a conscious effort to interact with speakers and fellow attendees. Grabbing photo opportunities was my ice-breaker. Those photos were not just keepsakes; they were gateways to potential collaborations.

4. Leveraging Social Media:

Post-event, those photographs became invaluable. Sharing them on social platforms allowed for continued interaction, tagging the influential figures and reminiscing about the shared moment. Social media acts as a bridge, turning fleeting encounters into sustained connections.

5. Building Bridges through Intermediaries:

Sometimes, directly connecting with an influential figure might be challenging. However, every influential person is surrounded by a team or 'handlers' who are more accessible. Building relationships with them can often be the stepping stone to getting closer to the figure themselves. My interactions at events often led me to connect with these intermediaries, who later played pivotal roles in securing influential guests for my podcast, FIVE Minute Bark.

6. Consistency is Key:

One-off interactions rarely yield lasting relationships. The key is consistent engagement. Whether it's commenting on their posts, sharing their content, or reaching out with meaningful messages, regular interactions ensure you remain on their radar.

Aligning with influential figures isn't about chasing fame. It's about recognizing the mutual value such associations can bring. My journey, from taking simple photos at an event to hosting influential figures on my podcast, underscores the power of authentic engagement. The next time you find yourself amidst potential influencers, remember that every big relationship starts with a small gesture. Seize the moment, engage genuinely, and watch as doors of unparalleled opportunities swing open.

Figure 1.11:

Align Yourself With The Right People

THE DOMINO EFFECT OF STRATEGIC CONNECTIONS

Opportunities often have a domino effect; one leads to another in an unending sequence, and before you realize it, you've paved a pathway to immense possibilities. My personal journey attests to this.

Securing an interview with Russell Brunson for his newly released book, "Expert Secrets," was a monumental milestone for me. If you're unfamiliar with him, Russell is a titan in the online marketing world and a leading figure in funnel building. To have him share insights for 40 minutes on my podcast, FIVE Minute Bark, was both nerve-wracking and exhilarating. The exchange went exceedingly well, and it added an invaluable feather to my cap.

This one interaction became a powerful conversational lever. When reaching out to other potential guests, especially those in Russell's orbit or who were aware of his prominence, the mere mention that I had interviewed him instantly elevated their perception of me. After all, they reasoned, if Russell found value in engaging with me, why shouldn't they? Aligning my podcast with someone of his stature became a potent endorsement.

The cascading benefits of this interaction were profound. My association with Russell and the ClickFunnels community deepened. I transitioned from being an admirer to an active participant, eventually getting personally invited to ClickFunnels headquarters. There, I underwent rigorous training to become a funnel builder and integrate my designs into their esteemed platform.

The ripple effects of these associations didn't stop there. Through a series of connected events and introductions, I found myself participating in Grant Cardone's "Ask The Pro" TV show. An encounter in the lobby led to an introduction to key personnel from Tony Robbins' team. This serendipitous meeting turned into an invitation to one of his esteemed events. That particular experience deserves its own narration and is a story I'll delve into in a forthcoming chapter.

The tapestry of these experiences underscores a profound truth: Every interaction, no matter how seemingly small, holds the potential to unlock doors you didn't even know existed. My journey from a podcast interview to elite training sessions, TV appearances, and serendipitous meetings is a testament to the infinite possibilities that await when you intentionally cultivate and nurture strategic relationships.

Figure 1.12:

WHY YOU SHOULD UNDERSTAND PODCASTING

AMPLIFY YOUR EXPERT: THE POWER OF BEING HEARD IN THE PODCAST WORLD

JOHN LEE DUMAS ON STAGE

My first encounter with podcasting was somewhat serendipitous, catalyzed by my friend Noah Wieder's invitation to a marketing event. At that time, I was grappling with uncertainty about my direction and purpose. Attempting to carve a niche in website design, I soon realized it wasn't my forte. Detail-oriented work demanded meticulous attention to layouts and content, and admittedly, my grammar skills were far from perfect. Despite the effectiveness of my websites, their glaring spelling and grammar errors didn't bother me much. I always figured that could be polished later by an expert, which eventually happened. But for other companies' websites, perfection was not just a desire but a necessity.

I've always admired bootstrap startups that prioritize launching over perfection, adhering to the belief that it's better to have something out there than nothing at all. Perfection can wait until revenue starts flowing in. However, after an encounter with an extremely particular client, I realized this approach wasn't universally applicable. Not everyone shared my perspective, and I found myself dreading the thought of undergoing such meticulous scrutiny again.

This marketing event became a turning point, especially when I listened to John Lee Dumas, a successful podcaster. His presentation was rich with insights, and he generously shared his blueprint for success in podcasting, starting with identifying the avatar and integrating it into a marketing plan. His approach resonated with me, and it sparked an epiphany. With my extensive experience as a BMX show rider and announcer, I realized that I could transition those skills to podcasting. Speaking live had always come naturally to me; why couldn't I channel that into a podcast?

At this juncture in my life, I was financially strained, navigating through dwindling savings and mounting bills. The prospect of podcasting felt like a lifeline, albeit a risky one. Friends and family were understandably concerned, and their worries were not unfounded. With overdue car payments, a looming mortgage, and a barrage of bills, the pressure was immense. But in my heart, I knew podcasting was my path forward. It was a "burn the boats" moment – a point of no return where I committed wholeheartedly to this new venture, fueled by a combination of desperation and conviction.

In hindsight, this leap into podcasting was not just a career move; it was a pivotal moment of reinvention. It was about harnessing my skills, experiences, and the lessons gleaned from years on the BMX circuit, and channeling them into a new form of expression and connection. This chapter of my life wasn't just about becoming a podcaster; it was about embracing change, facing risks, and finding a new way to share my voice with the world.

Why You Should Understand Podcasting

THE GIFT OF BEING A PODCAST GUEST

Imagine a room, packed with attentive listeners hanging onto your every word. Now, expand that room to a global audience, all plugged in, waiting to hear your story, your expertise. That's the power of being on a podcast. It's more than a conversation—it's an opportunity to share your narrative, your vision, and your passion.

I remember my initial podcast guesting experience vividly. The hum of the microphone, the expectant silence, and then the first question. As I spoke, I could feel connections being forged—listeners across the world nodding in agreement, jotting down notes, or simply being inspired. That one episode led to a spike in my website traffic, new followers, and countless messages from listeners who felt a connection with my journey.

But there's more to it than just the immediate benefits. Being a podcast guest refines your narrative. With every episode, every question, you refine your pitch, crystallize your thoughts, and reinforce your brand's message.

Why You Should Understand Podcasting

EMBARKING ON THE JOURNEY OF HOSTING

The allure of having my own podcast was irresistible. While being a guest offered a platform, having my own show was like building an empire. A space where I could set the tone, drive the narrative, and invite others to share their tales.

With each episode, I was not just a voice, but a curator of voices. And every guest that graced my show left behind a trail of listeners, curious to explore more. My website became more than just a digital business card—it transformed into a bustling hub of activity, all thanks to the organic traffic and backlinks generated through the podcast.

Your Voice, Your Echo, Your Legacy:

So, why am I sharing all this? Because I believe in the transformative power of podcasts. Whether you choose to step into the spotlight as a guest or take the helm as a host, there's an entire world out there, waiting to hear your voice.

If you've ever felt that you have a story worth sharing, insights worth spreading, or knowledge worth imparting, the podcast world is your oyster. Dive in, amplify your echo, and watch as the ripples spread far and wide, creating waves of impact and opportunities. Remember, in the vast digital landscape, your voice isn't just an asset—it's your legacy.

Figure 1.13:

Why You Should Understand Podcasting

STEPPING INTO THE SPOTLIGHT – MY PODCASTING ADVENTURE

With a plan firmly in hand, I embarked on the next chapter of my journey, drawing inspiration from Ron Stebenne's ethos: make it "PRO." It was time to level up, and for that, I turned to my trusted ally, Jason Malo. Together, we pooled resources to invest in top-of-the-line microphones. I knew that quality sound was non-negotiable; it's the Rolex of podcasting – an emblem of seriousness and style. Those mics weren't just tools; they were a symbol, a statement that I meant business.

I also gleaned wisdom from Mark Anthony about the importance of a professional backdrop. A step and repeat background was more than just a piece of fabric; it was a canvas that demanded attention. This single decision to go "PRO" paid dividends in respect and recognition. My guests would proudly share their photos on social media, flaunting those microphones and the backdrop. For many, these images became their chosen profile pictures. It was a hit, a visual testament to the professional standards I upheld.

But the real game-changer came unexpectedly. The "PRO" setup caught the eye of none other than Grant Cardone. Impressed by what he saw, he extended a personal invitation to his show. This was more than an opportunity; it was a validation of the path I had chosen.

As my podcasting journey progressed, it became clear that I was on to something big. I started attracting high-profile guests, gaining referrals and opening doors that previously seemed out of reach. The professional setup did more than just make my podcast look good; it positioned me in a space where I could connect, engage, and grow.

This chapter of my life was more than just about podcasting. It was a testament to the power of professionalism, the importance of presentation, and the impact of having the right tools. It was a journey of transforming from just another podcaster into a respected figure in the space, one interview at a time.

Figure 1.14:

Why You Should Understand Podcasting

QUALITY SOUND MATTERS

In the previous chapters, I've shared the pivotal moments in my journey to becoming a successful podcaster. One of the core strategies that propelled me to where I am today is what I like to call the "Go with a Pro" approach. It's not just a catchy phrase; it's a mindset and a set of actions that have transformed my podcasting venture into a resounding success. Now, I want to emphasize why you should consider adopting this approach for your own podcasting journey.

Quality Sound Matters The first pillar of the "Go with a Pro" approach is investing in top-of-the-line microphones. It might seem like a small detail, but in the world of podcasting, quality sound is paramount. When your audience hears your podcast, they want clarity, depth, and professionalism. Just as a Rolex watch catches the eye of a serious player or a discerning woman looking for a well-to-do man with style, these microphones are the symbol of your commitment to excellence. They signal to your listeners that you mean business and that you respect their time and attention.

Visual Impact Counts Another key element of the "Go with a Pro" approach is creating a visual impact. I learned from my good friend Mark Anthony that having a step and repeat backdrop is a must. It's a simple yet effective way to add professionalism to your podcast. When your guests step into your studio and see that backdrop, they know they're in a professional environment. This alone can earn you respect in the podcasting world.

Figure 1.17:

Leverage Social Proof One of the most remarkable outcomes of following the "Go with a Pro" approach was the power of social proof. When I implemented these strategies—investing in quality microphones and creating a professional visual setup—I noticed a significant change in the way my guests and audience perceived my podcast. My guests began sharing photos of themselves with those microphones and backdrop all over social media. Many even made these images their profile photos. The visual impact was so strong that it became a hit and generated tremendous social proof.

Leverage Social Proof Perhaps the most compelling reason to embrace the "Go with a Pro" approach is the way it can open doors to big opportunities. Thanks to the professional setup I had created, I gained the attention of influential figures in the podcasting world. As a result, Grant Cardone personally invited me to appear on his show because he was impressed by the level of professionalism I exhibited. This opportunity was a game-changer for my podcasting career.

Your Path to Success I want to emphasize that the "Go with a Pro" approach isn't just about looking the part; it's about creating an environment where success can flourish. By investing in quality sound, visual impact, and leveraging social proof, you can set yourself up for greatness in the world of podcasting. As I've experienced, this approach can lead to remarkable success and open doors you may have never imagined. So, if you're considering starting a podcast or looking to take your existing podcast to the next level, remember these key points and make the "Go with a Pro" approach an integral part of your journey. The results can be truly transformative.

Why You Should Understand Podcasting

KICKSTARTING YOUR PODCAST: A SIMPLE ROADMAP TO THE AIRWAVES

I'm about to share an outline of the steps I took to start my podcast. At first, it might seem overwhelming, considering all the technical details and subtle aspects of podcasting. However, the truth is, setting up your own podcast is actually quite straightforward. I'll provide you with a clear roadmap to get your podcast off the ground. The great news is, you might find yourself up and running much quicker than you anticipated.

1. Define Your Niche:
Before anything else, decide what your podcast will be about. Will it cater to a specific industry? Perhaps a personal passion or hobby? Pinpointing your niche will not only shape the content but attract a dedicated listener base.

2. Name & Branding:
Choose a catchy name for your podcast—one that's memorable and gives a hint of its content. Invest a bit of time (or money, if you're outsourcing) in creating a compelling logo or cover art. This becomes your podcast's visual identity.

3. Equipment & Software:

At its most basic, you'll need a good quality microphone and headphones. As for software, several user-friendly recording and editing tools are available, many of which are free or come at a nominal cost.

4. Recording:

Find a quiet place and start recording. If you're hosting interviews, platforms like Zoom or Skype can be valuable. Always do a soundcheck before you start to ensure clear audio.

5. Editing:

Post-production can polish your podcast. Cut out long pauses, "umms", or any unwanted segments. Add intro and outro music to give it a professional touch.

6. Hosting & Distribution:

Once your episode is ready, you need a podcast hosting platform. Sites like Libsyn, Podbean, or Anchor are excellent choices. From there, you can distribute your podcast to platforms like Apple Podcasts, Spotify, and Google Podcasts.

7. Promotion:

Share your episodes on social media, embed them on your website, or even create snippets or teasers to attract more listeners.

8. Consistency:
Remember, consistency is key in podcasting. Whether you release episodes weekly, bi-weekly, or monthly, ensure you maintain a schedule. It keeps your audience engaged and coming back for more.

The world of podcasting has democratized the voice—everyone can have a say. Within a few weeks or even days, you could have your voice resonating across continents, influencing thoughts, sparking debates, or simply entertaining. The question is, are you ready to hit the 'record' button?

PUBLIC SPEAKING AND GUEST SPEAKING

PLAYING GOD FOR A MOMENT

The journey to public speaking often begins in unexpected ways, in moments that demand sudden leaps from our comfort zones. My first true test as a speaker was not a deliberate step into the spotlight, but a necessity thrust upon me during my BMX school shows tour. Until that point, my voice was my bike—each jump, spin, and trick a sentence in a thrilling physical dialogue with the audience. My performance was a speech delivered through movement, my narrative spun with wheels and ramps.

But then came the day that would redefine my role. The lead speaker was unavailable, and there I was, the lead stunt rider, suddenly handed the microphone, not just to entertain but to communicate—a different kind of performance. The rush of executing a perfect sequence on the bike was familiar; the prospect of engaging a crowd with only my words was uncharted territory.

With little time to prepare, I scrambled together a list—a rudimentary script that would guide my impromptu debut. It was a makeshift lifeline, a series of bullet points to ensure I covered everything from safety tips to the importance of perseverance. Then, with a deep breath, I stepped forward to fill the silence.

As I spoke, I discovered a new dimension to my connection with the crowd. Without my bike as a mediator, I found rhythm in my voice, expression in pauses, and engagement in eye contact. The crowd's reactions were no longer just cheers for stunts well executed but nods of understanding, laughter at my quips, and the silent, focused attention that speakers crave.

This unexpected foray into public speaking taught me that the principles of a good BMX routine—timing, precision, practice—were not so different from those of a compelling speech. Both required an understanding of the audience, a clear objective, and the ability to adapt on the fly. The stunts that had once spoken for me had paved the way for a new means of expression.

Figure 1.21:

Public Speaking And Guest Speaking

THE STAGE CALLS TO ME

The stage calls to me now in a way that no ramp or bike ever could. With each opportunity to speak, there's an undeniable surge of adrenaline—a familiar echo of my BMX days, yet unique in its intensity. It's a cocktail of nerves and excitement, a reminder that I'm about to step into a transformative space. I know too well that the stage is a place where transformations happen, where a 'nobody' can become a 'somebody' through the sheer power of their words and the conviction in their delivery.

It's a daunting task, stepping out in front of an audience. The weight of their expectations can feel overwhelming, their attention a spotlight that's fixed solely on you. Yet, there's something about that moment that I've come to crave. Maybe it's the knowledge that words have the power to change lives, or the belief that even if I can't reach everyone, impacting just one person makes it all worthwhile.

Every time I stand before an audience, I aim to leave them with more than they came with—whether it's a new perspective, a renewed sense of purpose, or a call to action that resonates with their innermost aspirations. I've learned that striving to convert an entire crowd is an ambition that can dilute your message. Instead, I focus on the reachable few, those ready for change, those on the cusp of decision. This approach has never failed to steer my talks toward success.

In the midst of a speech, there's always a face in the crowd that stands out—the person who's truly listening, whose eyes reflect understanding or curiosity, who's perhaps nodding along or even showing skepticism. That's the person I talk to, the one I use as my anchor. By speaking to them, I find my flow, and that flow then ripples outward, touching the many, speaking to the collective.

Mastering the craft of public speaking is an ongoing journey, one that's as much about self-discovery as it is about conveying a message. It's in the intersection of vulnerability and strength that a speaker truly connects with their audience. Each speech is a performance, each word a stroke on the canvas, painting a picture that I hope will inspire, motivate, and awaken.

As you navigate through this part of my story, remember that public speaking is an art form that's accessible to all. It takes practice, patience, and a willingness to expose your heart to a room full of strangers. But the rewards—those moments when you know you've made an impact, however small—are incomparable. They're the moments when you realize that the craft you're mastering is not just about speaking well—it's about speaking meaningfully.

Figure 1.18:

Public Speaking And Guest Speaking

BE PLAYFUL

Embracing the spirit of playfulness on stage can transform the very nature of public speaking. Much like a rock star who teases and plays with the crowd, bringing them into the ebbs and flows of the performance, a speaker should also indulge in this dynamic exchange. It's in this playful space that the barrier between speaker and audience blurs, allowing for a connection that is both profound and genuine.

The stage is an extension of your personality, and it's crucial to bring your full self to it, awkward quirks and all. These idiosyncrasies make you relatable, grounding your speeches in reality and making them more accessible. Being playful means taking risks, trying out a new joke, or sharing a personal anecdote that may not always land perfectly. But it's in these moments, these attempts at something different, that your speeches come alive.

This playfulness also means being adaptive, reading the room, and being willing to deviate from the script when the opportunity for a genuine moment presents itself. Sometimes, the most memorable parts of a speech are unscripted—a spontaneous reaction to an audience member's comment, an improvised quip, or a moment of shared laughter. These instances can't be planned, but they can be embraced.

By allowing yourself to be playful, you invite your audience to be part of the experience rather than mere spectators. You're not just talking at them; you're talking with them, engaging in a dialogue that's both entertaining and enlightening. And as you become more comfortable with this playful approach, your speeches naturally evolve. They become more fluid, more engaging, and ultimately, more impactful.

The journey to becoming a masterful speaker is one of constant learning and adaptation. Playfulness is a tool in your arsenal, a way to keep your presentations fresh and your audience captivated. So, be bold, be spontaneous, and remember to enjoy the process. After all, if you're having fun on stage, chances are your audience is too, and that's when you know you're truly mastering the craft of public speaking.

Public Speaking And Guest Speaking

I KNOW PRACTICE MAKES PERFECT

When it comes to public speaking, the old adage that 'practice makes perfect' is more than just a saying—it's a fundamental truth. Every speech delivered, every presentation honed, and every audience interaction is a step closer to mastery, not just of the stage, but of your entire business narrative. The benefits that public speaking brings to your business and online presence are immeasurable and extend far beyond the applause at the end of a well-received talk.

As I ascended the ranks of my niche market, embracing the role of an expert, I discovered the symbiotic relationship between public speaking and my business's growth. Each opportunity to speak was a chance to refine my thoughts, to articulate my theories and to share industry secrets that I had learned on the front lines. The more I communicated, the more I understood the power of words—how they can shape a brand, define a mission, and persuade a crowd.

The reactions of a live audience are immediate and unfiltered. You can see understanding dawn on faces, witness the moment an idea resonates, or recognize when a point falls flat. This feedback is gold; it's a real-time barometer of your message's effectiveness. What makes the crowd lean in, what makes them nod, cheer, or inquire further—these reactions inform not just the content of your next speech but the content you produce for your online audience.

Suddenly, your SEO isn't just about keywords or search engine algorithms; it's about speaking directly to the heart of your audience's needs and interests. The topics that draw the loudest roars from the crowd are the ones you delve into deeper, both on stage and in the digital content you create. This isn't just throwing ideas against the wall to see what sticks—it's strategic, informed decision-making based on direct feedback.

This iterative process of testing and adjusting ensures that your products, services, and content are always in alignment with your audience's desires. It's a swift path to success, where the lag between idea and implementation is shortened, and your offerings are continually refined.

Public speaking has taught me that effective communication is an art—one that's perfected in the forge of experience. It's shown me that the lessons learned in front of a live audience are immediately applicable to my business's online strategy. The resonance of a crowd's reaction becomes the guidepost for my online content, steering the ship of my digital presence through the ever-changing seas of market demand.

As you absorb these insights, consider how your own experiences with public speaking, or any live audience engagement, can inform your business strategies. Recognize that your ability to communicate effectively in person is a powerful tool that, when translated to the digital realm, can elevate your brand and solidify your status as an expert in your field. Practice, indeed, makes perfect, and each practice session is an opportunity to not just become a better speaker, but a more attuned and responsive business owner.

CREATING YOUTUBE VIDEOS TO SUPPORT YOUR WEBPAGES

CRAFTING VIDEO OF YOUR EXISTING CONTENT

The written word is powerful. It forms the backbone of our websites, imparting knowledge, stirring emotions, and prompting action. But imagine if you could augment that strength, complementing it with a medium that is more dynamic, engaging, and caters to an audience that prefers seeing over reading? Welcome to the world of videos.

A picture is worth a thousand words, they say. If that's true, how much is a video worth? With the rapid rise of platforms like YouTube, Vimeo, and even TikTok, it's evident that videos have carved a significant niche in the digital realm. The reasons are manifold:

- Videos are digestible: In a fast-paced world, a concise, well-crafted video can convey information in minutes, which might take much longer to read.

- Videos cater to a broader audience: Not everyone enjoys reading. Some are visual learners who grasp concepts better when they see them in action.

- The human touch: Videos often allow viewers to connect on a personal level, seeing the face, hearing the voice, and feeling the passion behind the words.

So, how does this relate to your website content and 'more hands in the room'?

Think of videos as your website's dynamic alter ego. By repurposing your written content into video format, you're essentially casting a wider net, reaching out to both readers and viewers. Each video you create is similar to another hand raised in that grand ballroom, beckoning for attention but on a different platform – the world of video search engines and social media.

I embarked on this journey of transforming my written content into videos, and the results were enlightening. With every video echoing the sentiments of my written words, I was not only reinforcing my message but also ensuring that it reached those who might skip reading but would click on a video.

But it's not just about mere replication. The magic lies in adaptation. A good video version of your website content isn't a mere recitation; it's a reinterpretation. It brings in visual elements, voice modulations, animations, and possibly even testimonials or interviews. It takes the essence of your written word and presents it in a format that's tailor-made for visual consumption.

Diversifying into videos is not just a strategic move; it's a necessary one in today's digital age. Just as you'd diversify your financial investments, diversify your content mediums. The more varied and rich your content, the broader your reach. With every video rendition of your content, you're raising another hand, ensuring that in the vast digital room, you're impossible to overlook.

CREATING WEBINARS

THE WEBINAR

Webinars are the contemporary coliseums where businesses and thought leaders gather their audience not for a spectacle of combat but for a showcase of expertise, products, and services. In these digital arenas, the art of selling transforms; you're no longer an individual pitching to a single client across a table. Instead, you are the keynote speaker on a global stage, your voice reaching across continents in offices, living rooms, and coffee shops, your audience larger and more diverse than any physical venue could hold.

In the heart of this digital confluence is the power of the 'one-to-many' approach. Picture the traditional setting where sales are a painstaking process – a one-on-one meeting, a handshake, a look in the eye – all repeated as many times as there are potential clients. Now, replace that with a single webinar session. With the click of a button, you are transported into the lives of hundreds, perhaps thousands, ready to hear what you have to offer, ready to be convinced, ready to buy.

The persuasive power of a webinar lies in its inherent ability to tell a story, to weave the narrative of a product or service into the lives of those who listen. You're not merely listing features; you're demonstrating the transformative power of what you sell. You explain not just the 'how' but the 'why': why your product, why now, why their lives will be better for it. You are selling dreams, aspirations, and solutions.

In a webinar, your pitch can be as broad or as nuanced as you like. You might target a particular pain point common to your audience, address it with your offering, and then, like a skilled fisherman, reel your audience in with the promise of resolution. Or, you might cast a wider net, showcasing a suite of features, each a beacon calling to different segments of your audience, each finding resonance with individual needs and desires.

Moreover, webinars break down the barriers of time and place. In a physical sale, you and your potential client must both commit to a meeting, a slice of the day reserved for the dance of negotiation. In the digital world, a webinar transcends these constraints. It can be live, with the electric urgency of real-time interaction, or it can be recorded, watched at leisure, paused and contemplated, and then watched again. The sales pitch is no longer a fleeting moment but an enduring message, accessible at any time.

And the close? The moment of commitment in a webinar is both a personal and a communal experience. Calls to action are given with the excitement of a live audience, each individual feeling part of a larger movement, a shared journey with their fellow attendees. This creates a momentum, a wave of consensus that can encourage individuals to take the leap, to sign up, to purchase, to join the ranks of the convinced.

As we delve deeper into the anatomy of a successful webinar, remember this: the screen may separate you from your audience, but your ability to persuade, to inspire, and to sell remains as potent as ever. In the digital stage of webinars, you are not just a salesperson; you are a performer, and the world is your audience.

FINDING YOUR WAY

FIND YOUR WAY - THE ENTREPRENEUR'S JOURNEY THROUGH COMPLEXITY

Every entrepreneur's path is paved with untold complexity. In the beginning, there's often a spark—an idea that seems bright, feasible, and within reach. But as the journey unfolds, the path can become obscured by layers of unexpected challenges and intricacies that test the limits of your capabilities. Starting a software company, for instance, is a labyrinthine venture that I embarked on with a mix of naivety and audacity. If I had known the depth of technical knowledge required, the intricate web of coding, the delicate interplay of features and updates, perhaps I would have hesitated. But it's the not knowing, sometimes, that allows us to leap.

In the crucible of development and deployment, I learned that even the most seemingly benign updates could unravel functioning parts of the software, like a thread pulled inadvertently that loosens the entire tapestry. These moments of error, often invisible to the creator's eye yet glaring to the new user, are humbling. They remind you that the system you've built, much like the process of building it, is not infallible. As the users navigate, they may stumble upon these errors, each misstep a beacon highlighting a flaw I never saw, each ticket raised a lesson in humility and resilience.

Navigating through these challenges, the unwinding of issues that can stretch for hours, even days, becomes a testament to perseverance. There's a peculiar solace in the cycle of breakage and repair, a rhythm that becomes familiar, almost comforting. With every problem that arises, you learn to trust that solutions will emerge—that the dawn will bring problem-solving clarity. This trust is hard-earned, a product of repeated trials and tribulations that fortify your resolve.

This book is not just a guide; it's a reassurance. It's a message that says, "You're not alone on this journey." The obstacles you encounter, the doubts that assail you, the processes that seem insurmountably flawed—they're all part of the terrain of entrepreneurship. Your path, with all its unique trials and errors, is yours alone. It's a process that's being perfected in real-time, with each decision, each failure, and each success.

Indeed, it can be tempting to look over the fence at someone else's journey, to wonder if adopting their methods would make the path smoother. But the truth is, adopting someone else's process wholesale is like wearing clothes tailored for another—you might get by, but they'll never fit quite right. Instead, gather wisdom from others like pieces of a map; use them to navigate, but do not let them dictate your path. Your process, with all its madness and mayhem, is the crucible in which your entrepreneurial spirit is tested and tempered.

As you continue to forge ahead, remember that the flawed process is not a sign of defeat but a hallmark of the entrepreneurial spirit. It is a rite of passage that shapes your venture and yourself. In the end, it's the journey that matters—the relentless pursuit, the undying quest for improvement, and the personal growth that comes with it. Embrace your process, flawed as it may be, for it is the making of you and your business.

INCEPTION OF RANKINGMASTERY

Embarking on a mission to secure a stable income, I circled back to my foundational passion - organizing BMX shows. This undertaking was akin to starting from scratch, posing a formidable test of my capabilities. My task was to establish a business from nothing, devoid of leads or a pre-laid foundation. This phase was more than a mere challenge; it was an opportunity for rediscovery and innovation, compelling me to delve into new strategies and tools for success.

My familiarity with the BMX business was unparalleled, and I had confidence in my unmatched expertise. My strategy involved leveraging SEO by creating landing pages for all the keyword sets that had previously benefited me and were still profitable for the company I had sold. This task was exhaustive, involving manual labor to create individual pages, each tailored to different keyword phrases. Although writing content wasn't exactly my forte, I operated under the belief that having something, no matter how imperfect, was better than nothing. With unwavering dedication, I devoted days to crafting 10 to 20 pages, each uniquely optimized to rank well in search engines.

Inception Of RankingMastery

THE ONLINE DIRECTORY STRATEGY

In my relentless pursuit of generating leads, I stumbled upon what seemed at first like a hair-brain idea – creating an online directory featuring all my competitors. This concept was inspired by the observation that directories often enjoy higher rankings in search engine results. Consider the dominance of platforms like Yelp and other similar services; they seemingly have a monopoly on the top positions in online searches.

My goal was to tap into this trend. By creating a directory, I wasn't just looking to list businesses; I was aiming to carve out a space in the highly competitive digital landscape. The directory would not only serve as a resource for potential clients looking for BMX shows but also position my own services strategically within that space.

This approach was unconventional, especially considering that it involved promoting my competitors. However, the idea was rooted in the belief that by providing value and a comprehensive view of the market, I would draw more traffic to the directory.

More traffic could mean higher visibility for my own offerings, indirectly benefiting from the collective presence of all listed competitors.

Embracing this strategy, I embarked on developing the directory, fully aware of the challenges it posed yet excited by its potential to disrupt the conventional approach to lead generation and online presence.

With the concept of the online directory in hand, I plunged into action. My mission was clear: to create a searchable directory optimized with all the keyword phrases relevant to my business. I was racing against the clock, as financial pressures mounted and bills piled up. This period in my life was more than just stressful; it was a test of endurance, both mentally and physically.

Each day was a battle against overwhelming odds. The pressure was tangible, with every moment feeling like a delicate balancing act. I often found myself moving through my tasks with a methodical slowness, taking measured breaths, and focusing intently on each action to prevent myself from being overwhelmed by the situation. The possibility of fainting from sheer stress loomed over me like a dark cloud.

Despite the immense pressure, I was driven by a sense of urgency and purpose. Knowing that every step taken was a step closer to financial stability and professional success kept me going. I meticulously built the directory, ensuring it was not just comprehensive but also user-friendly and optimized for search engines.

This part of my journey was far from easy. It required not just technical skills and marketing know-how but also a resilience of spirit. The directory project became more than just a business strategy; it became a symbol of my fight against adversity, a concrete manifestation of my determination to succeed against all odds.

Inception Of RankingMastery

THE UNEXPECTED TURN

As I worked feverishly through the holiday season, I clung to the hope that by January, I could capitalize on the usual rush of bookings that come at the start of the year. The BMX show industry has its rhythms, with peak seasons from January to March and then August to mid-October. Knowing this, I felt my efforts could soon pay off, provided I timed everything perfectly. My directory was now operational and searchable, thanks to the assistance of a resourceful assistant from the Philippines who helped populate it with a comprehensive list of acts.

But then came an oversight that I hadn't anticipated. In my rush and focus on building the directory, I had neglected one crucial aspect: seeking consent from the companies before listing them. Operating under the assumption that they could always opt-out later, I hadn't foreseen the repercussions of this decision. What harm could it do, I thought? After all, more exposure is always good, isn't it?

Early January brought a harsh reality check. My inbox, which I hoped would contain inquiries and booking confirmations, instead held a series of cease and desist letters from lawyers. The accusations were straightforward: I had added companies to my directory without permission, and to make matters worse, my directory listings were outranking their original websites on Google. This meant that their potential clients were being redirected to my platform instead of theirs.

The severity of the situation hit me like a ton of bricks. I had inadvertently stepped into a legal minefield, and the stress of the potential consequences was overwhelming. The fear of legal action and the potential financial implications were a significant blow. It felt like the final straw, a catastrophic end to my painstaking efforts. The thought that kept circling in my mind was, "This is it. I'm finished."

Inception Of RankingMastery

THE MIRACLE SHOWER REVELATION

That day, as I moved away from the overwhelming reality of my computer screen, I headed towards a place of clarity and solace - my shower. I often refer to it as the "Miracle Shower." Over the years, it's been the birthplace of numerous groundbreaking ideas, providing a sanctuary where clarity emerges amidst the cascade of warm water. It's a space where solutions seem to materialize, transforming challenges into opportunities.

As the water flowed, my mind raced with negative thoughts, replaying the morning's daunting emails. Yet, in that space of solitude and reflection, a transformative thought struck me, as clear and forceful as the water itself. It was an 'aha' moment, a realization borne out of the chaos of the morning's events - a clear manifestation of the 'treasure map mode' in action.

The reality hit me like a wave: I had developed a software that could rank someone on Google. It wasn't just any ordinary directory; it was a framework, a meticulously designed tool that had proven its capability to rank businesses effectively. And these were merely directory listings, not even full-fledged website pages. A revelation washed over me, bringing with it a sense of excitement and hope. I found myself exclaiming aloud, "This works! This really works!"

In that moment, the pieces of the puzzle began to fit together. The cease and desist letters, the stress, and the challenges - they were all indicators of the software's potential. It was a testament to its power and efficacy in the digital realm. If this directory, a side aspect of my project, could achieve such results, imagine what tailored, individual website pages could accomplish.

This shower epiphany marked a pivotal turning point. It was a moment of transformation, where despair turned into determination. I realized that the tool I had developed could be a game-changer, not just for directory listings but for any business, including my own. The potential was vast and untapped, waiting to be explored and utilized.

As I stepped out of the shower, I felt a renewed sense of purpose and direction. The challenge now was to harness this potential, to refine and adapt the software for broader applications. This was the birth of a new chapter, a chapter where the focus shifted from despair to development, from problem to potential. The path ahead was clear: it was time to unlock the full capabilities of this software and introduce it to the world. The journey of RankingMastery was about to take a significant leap forward.

Inception Of RankingMastery

THE EXPANSION OF POSSIBILITIES

In the aftermath of the 'Miracle Shower' revelation, I began to see the directory I had created in a new light. Initially, my intention was straightforward: build a directory to generate leads for my BMX shows. But now, I realized I had inadvertently stumbled upon a powerful SEO tool, one with potential far beyond my original plans.

The directory was more than a list of names and services; it was a searchable database with rich, varied attributes. Each performer had an account featuring images, categories, and specific details like educational levels, states of performance, and types of messages delivered. This level of detail meant that every entry was not just a listing but a unique, searchable entity. Performers could be found based on state, message type, school grade level, and even the style of their show. Each of these attributes made every page distinct and indexable by Google. The implications were staggering.

As I delved deeper into this realization, a world of possibilities began to unfold. If every unique combination of attributes could generate a separate page that Google would index, then the potential for SEO was immense. We were no longer talking about ranking 20 pages; this could lead to hundreds, even thousands of individually ranked pages. The thought was exhilarating.

The key to unlocking this potential lay in the database. If I could set it up to dynamically replace content on each page based on the selected keyword phrases, the impact could be groundbreaking. This was more than just a directory; it was a prototype for an SEO juggernaut.

I began to envision a system where each page was not only unique but optimized for search engines. Every state, every school type, every message, and every show type could have its dedicated, SEO-friendly page. This meant unparalleled visibility and a level of customization in SEO that was rarely seen.

The excitement of this discovery fueled my drive. I was no longer just trying to salvage a business or escape financial duress; I was on the verge of creating something revolutionary in the SEO world. The directory had laid the groundwork, but the real journey was just beginning. It was time to harness this concept and scale it up. I was ready to take this accidental discovery and turn it into a deliberate strategy for success. The path to RankingMastery was becoming clearer, and I was ready to embark on this new, promising journey.

Part 7: Realizing the Full Potential

As I stood at the precipice of this new revelation, the focus shifted from salvaging a directory to revolutionizing my website. The potential I had stumbled upon was not just an incremental improvement but a complete transformation of how content could be dynamically presented and ranked on search engines. It was time to apply this breakthrough to my BMX show website, turning it into a testbed for what would eventually become RankingMastery.

The concept was simple yet profound. For instance, if I targeted a specific niche like 'drug awareness messages for elementary schools in California,' I could tailor every aspect of a webpage to align precisely with that theme. The possibilities were limitless. I could configure pages to display content, pricing structures, images, and even videos, all meticulously tailored to match the specific keyword phrase. This customization was achieved through a network of relational IDs in the database, linking each piece of content to its corresponding search term.

This approach was groundbreaking. The idea of having web pages that could morph based on specific search criteria was akin to watching a chameleon change colors – a digital metamorphosis that was both fascinating and incredibly efficient. What previously took hours of manual labor could now be accomplished with a few strategic database entries. Each page could transform to showcase precisely what the target audience was searching for, dramatically increasing the relevance and, by extension, the potential for higher search engine rankings.

Watching pages evolve and adapt in real-time was not just innovative; it was exhilarating. It felt like witnessing the birth of the telephone – a moment where you realize that the world as you know it has changed. This wasn't just about creating SEO-friendly pages; it was about redefining the very nature of how websites could interact with search engines and users.

This period marked a significant turning point. I was no longer just a BMX show organizer; I was on the verge of becoming a pioneer in SEO and web development. My website became a living laboratory, constantly evolving and improving as I refined the system. This was the inception of what RankingMastery would become – a tool that could transform any website into a dynamic, SEO-optimized powerhouse. The journey from a struggling entrepreneur to an innovator in digital marketing was underway, and I was ready to see just how far this new path could take me.

Inception Of RankingMastery

VISION BECOMES REALITY

As my experimentation with this novel concept began to stabilize, a realization dawned on me. This wasn't just a groundbreaking approach for my BMX show website; it was a scalable, adaptable formula that could revolutionize how any company approached website creation and SEO. The prospect of transforming this personal tool into a universal solution was both thrilling and daunting.

The idea was clear: develop a platform that allowed any business to leverage this technology, creating web pages that were not only aesthetically pleasing but also finely tuned for search engine optimization based on specific keywords and content relevant to their industry. This platform would empower businesses to make dynamic websites that could adapt and evolve, just like mine had.

But what to name this brainchild? The naming process is always a blend of creativity and intuition, trying to encapsulate the essence of the product in a word or two. After much brainstorming and discarding several potential names, my friend David Holden suggested "RankingMastery." It was perfect – the name not only conveyed the core functionality of the platform but also its ultimate goal: mastering the art of ranking on search engines. I hurriedly checked the domain availability, and to my delight, it was there for the taking. RankingMastery.com was soon mine.

Registering the domain felt like a ceremonial step, an official christening of a new venture. RankingMastery was no longer just an idea or a personal project; it had a name, an identity, and a potential that stretched far beyond my initial vision. This platform was to be a game-changer, a tool that would shift the focus from mere web design to content-driven, SEO-optimized web development.

This pivotal moment marked the transition from a concept to a tangible product. RankingMastery was set to become more than a tool; it was a philosophy, a new approach to web presence. It was about empowering businesses, regardless of their size or industry, to harness the power of SEO and truly master their online ranking.

The journey ahead was filled with challenges and opportunities, but the path was clear. RankingMastery was poised to change the way businesses approached their online presence, offering a smarter, more strategic way to connect with their audience and dominate search engine rankings. The vision was set, and it was time to bring RankingMastery to the world.

Inception Of RankingMastery

EXPANDING HORIZONS

With RankingMastery transitioning from a concept to a working model, the next phase of development presented a unique set of challenges. The task at hand was to scale the platform, making it versatile and user-friendly for a wide array of businesses. This stage was critical – it involved conceptualizing and implementing features that would allow users to create, edit, and manage their websites effectively through RankingMastery.

The journey of scaling this software was akin to navigating uncharted waters. Every decision, from the layout of user accounts to the intricacies of website editing tools, was crucial. The goal was to create a platform that not only served my business's needs but could be easily adapted to fit the diverse requirements of multiple clients.

Thankfully, the BMX show bookings, now bolstered by my strong online presence, were generating steady revenue. This financial breathing room was invaluable, as it allowed me to focus my energies on evolving RankingMastery. The automated systems I had put in place for the BMX business meant I could devote more time to this new venture, turning my full attention to the development and refinement of the software.

Piece by piece, the platform began to take shape. I introduced features that would allow for separate client accounts, each with their own login and customization options. This was a significant milestone – it meant that RankingMastery was no longer just a tool for my use but a versatile platform that could cater to a variety of businesses.

Embracing this challenge, I onboarded my first few clients, each with their unique needs and visions for their websites. This initial phase was both exhilarating and daunting. Every client presented an opportunity to test and refine the capabilities of RankingMastery, pushing the software to its limits and beyond.

As the software began to take on real clients, I found myself not just as a developer, but as a facilitator of online success for other businesses. Each successful website build was a testament to the platform's potential and a step closer to realizing the vision of RankingMastery as a leading SEO and website development tool.

This period was more than just about building a software; it was about laying the groundwork for a new era of digital marketing. RankingMastery was poised to empower businesses to take control of their online presence, to master the art of ranking, and to thrive in the competitive digital landscape.

The real journey of RankingMastery had begun, and with each new client, the platform evolved, grew stronger, and moved closer to becoming a pivotal tool in the realm of SEO and online marketing.

Expanding Horizons

UTILIZING NEW PLATFORMS FOR GROWTH

With RankingMastery ready for a wider audience, and my podcast, which had now featured over 400 interviews, gaining momentum, it was the perfect opportunity to synergize these two ventures. The respect and recognition I had garnered from the podcast provided a unique platform to introduce RankingMastery to an audience already engaged and interested in expanding their online presence.

I decided to leverage this built-in audience by hosting webinars that not only showcased my expertise in digital marketing but also demonstrated the capabilities and benefits of RankingMastery. This approach was strategic, tapping into an existing network of professionals and entrepreneurs who were already familiar with my work and trusted my judgment.

The initial webinars were a learning experience. Each session improved from the last, as I fine-tuned the presentation, addressed audience questions, and showcased real-time examples of how RankingMastery could enhance their online visibility.

The feedback was invaluable; it not only helped in refining the webinar format but also provided insights into the specific needs and challenges faced by potential clients.

This direct interaction with the audience was crucial. It helped in understanding the nuances of their online marketing needs, which in turn allowed for continuous improvement and adaptation of RankingMastery. The webinars became a key tool in both educating potential users about SEO and demonstrating the practical applications of RankingMastery in achieving their digital marketing goals.

As the webinars gained traction, so did the interest in RankingMastery. Prospective clients began to see the value in a platform that could simplify and streamline their SEO efforts. The realization that there were still gaps in the software was apparent, but it was also clear that these could be addressed over time. The main focus was on the core value RankingMastery offered – the ability to significantly improve online visibility and ranking.

This period marked a significant shift in my journey. I was no longer just a podcast host or a former BMX rider; I had become a facilitator of online growth, helping others harness the power of the internet to elevate their businesses. The synergy between the podcast and RankingMastery was a testament to the power of leveraging multiple platforms to build a cohesive and powerful brand presence.

The journey of RankingMastery was now in full swing, driven by the dual engines of a successful podcast and an innovative software platform. Each webinar brought new clients and new challenges, but more importantly, it solidified RankingMastery's position as a viable, valuable tool in the competitive world of online marketing.

Expanding Horizons

ADDRESSING CLIENT NEEDS AND SOFTWARE LIMITATIONS

As RankingMastery's client base expanded, so did the variety and complexity of their demands. Each request brought with it the opportunity to enhance the software, though not without its share of challenges. Some updates, seemingly straightforward, would inadvertently trigger errors in other parts of the system, revealing vulnerabilities I hadn't anticipated. These moments were a mix of embarrassment and stress, yet they were also invaluable learning experiences.

The growing pains of RankingMastery were, in essence, a reflection of its success. Every glitch uncovered by a client was a chance to improve, and every feedback was a step towards refinement. The most crucial lesson I learned during this phase was the importance of listening to the client's needs. It became clear that the path to a truly great product wasn't about what I thought the clients needed, but about genuinely understanding and delivering what they actually wanted.

One of the significant hurdles that emerged was the limitation regarding domain attachment. Initially, clients could only use the RankingMastery.com domain, which, while functional, lacked the appeal and personalization that many desired. This limitation was a frequent point of objection during client discussions, and I knew addressing it would not only enhance the software's capabilities but also boost its marketability.

Navigating this challenge required a deep dive into the technical framework of RankingMastery. The goal was to enable clients to attach their domains to their sites, giving them the autonomy and brand identity they sought. This feature was more than just a technical upgrade; it was a critical step in legitimizing RankingMastery as a versatile and professional SEO tool.

The process was arduous, filled with technical hurdles and long nights. But the result was worth every effort. Once the domain attachment feature was successfully integrated and rolled out, the response from clients was overwhelmingly positive. It was a turning point that not only elevated the software's status but also reinforced my commitment to continuous improvement and client satisfaction.

This chapter in the journey of RankingMastery highlighted the dynamic nature of software development and the importance of adaptability. It was a testament to the fact that challenges, when embraced and addressed head-on, pave the way for growth and success. The evolution of RankingMastery, driven by client feedback and technical innovation, was shaping it into a tool that not only met but exceeded client expectations, setting a new standard in the SEO software landscape. doesn't

INTRODUCTION TO RANKINGMASTERY SOFTWARE PLATFORM

DISCOVER THE EFFICIENCY OF RANKINGMASTERY

As you turn the pages of this book, absorbing the intricate dance of RankingMastery, you've journeyed through a transformative understanding of SEO, personal branding, and digital marketing. Now, at the culmination of this voyage, it's time to unveil how you can apply all these learnings with unparalleled efficiency and effectiveness using RankingMastery.

The RankingMastery Way: A Path to Accelerated Success

Imagine the time and effort you'd typically invest in creating an SEO-optimized page – selecting keywords, styling text, managing meta tags, and more. Now, envision accomplishing all these tasks in a fraction of the time with RankingMastery.

Speed and Simplicity in SEO: A Real-World Scenario

Let's put RankingMastery to the test:

- Select a Keyword Phrase: Your journey begins with choosing the right keyword phrase.

- Create Your Content: Craft content that speaks to your audience and aligns with your SEO goals.

- Enter the World of RankingMastery: Here, simplicity meets innovation.

- Effortless Integration: Add your keyword phrase and attach your content document.

- Instantaneous Transformation: Click "add" and witness your content come alive on your website.

But there's more:

- Forget manual content distribution throughout the site – RankingMastery does it for you.

- No more fussing over text styling – it's all pre-set to your brand's aesthetics.

- Metadata, image tags, schema for Google – all handled seamlessly.

- Even internal linking and content relation – effortlessly managed.

THE STORY OF TRANSFORMATION: RANKINGMASTERY 2.0

Let's delve into a success story. An enterprise, previously dedicating 160 hours to create 85 landing pages, embraced RankingMastery 2.0. The result? A complete web overhaul in just 6 hours, with each page finely tuned for individual keyword phrases. This is the magic of RankingMastery – blending efficiency with efficacy.

AI-POWERED SEO OPTIMIZATION: A TOOL THAT WORKS WHILE YOU SLEEP

RankingMastery's AI-driven platform redefines optimization. It crafts perfect SEO pages autonomously, allowing you to focus on broader strategic goals while your website climbs the SEO ladder, effortlessly.

AN ENTREPRENEUR'S DREAM: THE ALL-IN-ONE SEO WEBSITE BUILDER

For small businesses and entrepreneurs, RankingMastery is a game-changer. It's not just a tool; it's a partner in your quest for digital visibility and business growth.

TESTIMONIAL: A STORY OF IMMEDIATE IMPACT

Jason Malo of Advanced Auto, Inc. shares, "Google Organic Search accounts for 80% of our new customers. It's astonishing – three websites built with RankingMastery hit Page 1 of Google in days. What used to cost us thousands now brings quicker, more impactful results."

As you step into the world of applied SEO and digital marketing mastery, remember that RankingMastery is more than a platform; it's your ally in the digital realm. It's time to move beyond traditional methods and embrace the future – a future where efficiency, efficacy, and success are not just goals but realities.

Welcome to the RankingMastery way – where your journey in mastering the digital world reaches new heights of efficiency and effectiveness.

CONCLUSION

THE CONVINCING ARGUMENT

As we journeyed together through the intricacies of optimizing, ranking, branding, and expanding our digital footprint, one common theme emerged - the importance of having the right tools to achieve our goals. Let's take a moment to reflect on our shared voyage and see why, at its culmination, the answer for many is resoundingly: RankingMastery.

- Understanding the Digital World's Hierarchies: We unveiled the parallels between societal networks and the digital realm. Like the influential individuals in society, certain websites hold significant clout in the digital space. Being associated or linked by these giants can skyrocket your site's credibility and ranking. This isn't so different from being invited to an exclusive event by someone prominent.

- Real Estate in the Digital Realm: Just as the value of a physical property appreciates over time, so does the digital 'plot' your website occupies. With effort and optimization, a high search ranking becomes similar to a prime property in the heart of a bustling city - immensely valuable.

- More Hands in the Room: We've explored the power of maximizing our presence, increasing our chances of being seen and heard. Be it in a seminar or the vast realm of Google search, having 'more hands in the room' (or more web assets in search) amplifies our visibility and opportunities.

- Venturing into Videos: By transforming written content into dynamic videos, we're catering to a broader audience, ensuring our message resonates across different platforms, especially with the visually inclined.

Now, how does one streamline these insights, ensuring every aspect is catered to without being overwhelmed? Enter RankingMastery. This isn't just another platform; it's your strategic partner in achieving online prominence.

Here's the undeniable value RankingMastery offers:

- Dynamic Page Creation: With the capability to dynamically generate pages optimized for search indexing, RankingMastery stands leagues ahead. It's like having an architect who knows precisely how to design every room of a house to perfection.

- Time Efficiency: Why spend countless hours tinkering when you can achieve results in a fraction of the time? RankingMastery's tools are geared to fast-track your digital success.

- Mobile Optimization: In an era where mobile browsing is paramount, the platform ensures your pages are mobile-ready with minimal adjustments.

- Designer's Delight: Envision a haven where the robustness of Photoshop meets the versatility of web design. This platform is that haven.

- Content Libraries: An organized, easily accessible repository for all your assets. Think of it as your digital wardrobe, where everything is neatly arranged, ready to be donned.

- AI Integration: Content that's not only rich but also uniquely tailored to your business. It's like having a personal scribe who knows your voice and crafts messages perfectly aligned with your brand.

- Expansion Tools: Whether you're branching into course creation, book writing, or other ventures, RankingMastery evolves with you, offering tools to support your growth.

RankingMastery isn't just a tool; it's a revolution. Built from the ground up by experts who understand the intricacies of SEO and design, it aims to give every user - from startups to conglomerates - an unparalleled edge in the digital domain. As we close this chapter, remember: in the realm of digital ranking, with RankingMastery, you're not just playing the game; you're mastering it.

Conclusion

OUR JOURNEY TOGETHER

As we approach the final pages of this journey together, let's take a moment to reflect on the paths we've traversed and the insights we've gained. You, the reader, have been invited into a narrative that intertwines the principles of SEO with the larger tapestry of life's endeavors. From the earliest anecdotes of childhood creativity and determination, to the adrenaline-fueled world of BMX, and into the intricate dance of entrepreneurship and online influence, each chapter has aimed to equip you with the tools to carve out your own success.

You've learned that mastery is not a destination but a process—a continual striving for excellence that spans both the digital realm and the personal spheres of our lives. You've discovered that the strategies which propel us to the top of search engine rankings can also elevate our personal and professional relationships, and that the agility required to navigate the ever-changing algorithms of online platforms is similar to adapting to life's unpredictable challenges.

We've delved into the art of public speaking, the thrill of connecting with an audience, and the power of a well-told story.

You've seen how the authenticity of a speaker can mirror the authenticity we strive for in our online content, and how the same principles that make for compelling speeches can be applied to create engaging, search-optimized material.

You've witnessed the symbiosis between the experiences of our past and the potential of our future, understanding that every skill acquired, every obstacle overcome, and every moment of joy experienced can be a stepping stone towards greater achievements.

This book has been a call to action—a reminder that each day presents new opportunities to rank higher not just in the virtual world, but in the reality of our life's pursuits. The 'cause of accomplishment' is a multifaceted one, driven by a combination of passion, persistence, and the willingness to learn and adapt.

As you step beyond this final chapter, remember that the mastery you seek, whether in SEO, in life, or in the influence you wish to wield, is within your grasp. The lessons imparted here are your tools; how you use them will shape the narrative of your success.

Conclusion

THE FINAL CHAPTER OF THIS BOOK

As we close the final chapter of this book, it's not the end but an invitation to an ongoing adventure. The principles, strategies, and personal anecdotes shared within these pages are just the beginning. I am excited to offer you the opportunity to deepen your understanding and application of everything we've covered through an expansive course that further delves into online search, podcasting, marketing, networking, and public speaking—all integral components of a successful digital presence.

This course is designed as a comprehensive roadmap, guiding you through the practical implementation of the concepts we've explored. But the journey doesn't stop with theory and practice alone. To truly revolutionize how you approach the digital landscape, I've channeled all these insights into the creation of the RankingMastery Software platform.

RankingMastery isn't just another tool—it's the embodiment of efficiency and effectiveness, crafted to save you thousands of hours while managing your online presence. This platform is unique, conceived from firsthand experience and tailored to the needs of anyone looking to make a significant impact online. With it, you can swiftly execute the strategies we've discussed, and manage expansive pages of content—something that would be overwhelmingly complex with any other software.

I warmly invite you to continue this journey with me. Let's take the knowledge you've gained and put it into action, harnessing the power of RankingMastery to elevate your online search rankings, to amplify your voice through podcasting, to refine your marketing, to forge powerful alliances, and to captivate audiences from any stage.

The pathway to mastery is not walked alone, and I am here to accompany you every step of the way. Let's embark on this next phase together, and witness the transformation of your digital influence into tangible, rewarding success. Welcome to the ongoing journey of mastery.

ACKNOWLEDGMENTS

ACKNOWLEDGEMENTS

I am immensely grateful to the multitude of people who have been a part of my life, offering their perspectives, listening intently, and collaborating with me. The ideas and strategies that fill the pages of this book have been inspired by these interactions. I extend my heartfelt thanks to all my current and past colleagues and friends who have been instrumental in helping me test and refine these ideas, and for their contributions to my journey of trials and triumphs.

I have been deeply inspired by many marketers, notably Steve Olsher and Russell Brunson, whose insights have been invaluable in my learning process.

To my friends and support group, thank you for being there every step of the way. While I will attempt to acknowledge everyone and give credit where it's due, I apologize in advance if I inadvertently miss anyone. In no particular order, I want to express my gratitude to:

My loving family – Joan, Herve, Jimmy, Jill, Betsy, and Susan. Your unwavering support has been my stronghold. To my friends – Jewels Arnes, Jack Barnes, Gretchen & Matt Bergman, Scott

Moroney, Jim Case, Mark Anthony, Cameron Czubernat, Deborah Sauter, Peter & Paul Davidson, David Holden, Dasha Green, Larry Gregerson, Dean Hecker, Woody Itson, Lauren Jackson, Kevin Levine, Karl Zeilik, Goss Lindsey, Tony Peloquin, Jason Malo, Noah Wieder, Wayne Meyers, Danny & the Moreno family, Richard Mostowy, Eric Nielsen, Michael O'Neal, Matt Salmon, Darren Pelio, Kelly Poelker, Darren Prescott, Ron Stebenne, Jeff Repetto, David Rosen, Nate Shevlin, Jeff Smith, Robert Smith, Jason Stroder, Blair Williams, Jeff Winston, Sam Wolanyk, Florian Zerhusen, and the many others who have been a part of my incredible journey.

Your contributions, big or small, have shaped my path and for that, I am forever grateful.

ABOUT THE AUTHOR

ABOUT THE AUTHOR

Dennis Langlais' extraordinary journey from a world-class professional BMX Freestyler to a digital marketing and entrepreneurship maven is nothing short of inspiring. His BMX career, marked by international tours and visits to every state in the USA, not only brought him notable success but also played a pivotal role in popularizing the sport. Shifting gears, Dennis then brought his dynamic energy and passion for performance to the online business arena. He launched the "FIVE Minute Bark" podcast, conducting over 300 interviews, and established himself as a voice of influence and insight. Dennis is also the creative force behind "RankingMastery," an innovative software platform that empowers individuals and businesses to enhance their online presence.

His book, "RankingMastery: The Cause of Accomplishment," merges the wisdom gained from his sports career with actionable digital marketing strategies. Dennis's journey, characterized by resilience, adaptability, and an unwavering commitment to success, positions him as an influential mentor and source of inspiration for aspiring entrepreneurs and digital marketers.

Figure 1.15: